# What others say about *"Let's Connect!"*

"It takes insight and action to be a great networker. *"Let's Connect!"* gives valuable insight and offers action steps that enable you to stay in touch with people in a way that is effective, efficient, and fun. I highly recommend this book."

**Dr. Ivan Misner,** Founder of BNI, networking author, columnist and speaker, www.bni.com.

"The first time I met Jan Vermeiren, I was charmed by his sincerity and drive to help people to network. Jan's vision is that networking is not about accumulating power or creating self-importance, but about helping each other by sharing, learning and supporting. In *"Let's Connect!"* Jan reveals tips and to do's that are very interesting to read for everyone, but more importantly he describes a different kind of networking. It's not about 'me, myself and I' - but about helping others and giving without expecting something in return."

**Bart Becks,** CEO Belgacom Skynet, www.skynet.be

"This book is right in line with the "Relationship first, business second" motto that we have on Ecademy. If you want to know what networking really is about and learn how to network in a fun, rewarding and efficient way, don't just read this book, but apply its wisdom in practice!"

**Thomas Power,** chairman Ecademy, www.ecademy.com

"Networking is more than a technique; it's a way of living. This book really guides and coaches you in crossing your personal barriers and just going out there and "connecting." It shows how networking can help you to get the most of your contacts and potential contacts and most of all: that it is important to give and receive."

**Inge Dom,** HR Business Partner at Alcatel, www.alcatel.com

"This book reads like a train even if you're not a native English speaker. It is a keep-me-at-hand and think-and-do-book that is a token of respect for human kind and fellow men."

***Tine Demeester***, Director VKW Brabant, www.vkw.be

"Networking is not a synonym for the favorite leisure activity of yups and directors or top officials at the end of their career. Adult networks provide competitive advantages to any decision maker, for himself and for his company. And, if you are still in doubt: networking is about working to achieve a specific goal. Accidental one shots do not give you anything. Therefore, *"Let's Connect!"*" is an indispensable guide."

***Peter Van Sande***, Director Networking and Services, Voka - Kamer van Koophandel (Chamber of Commerce) Limburg, www.kvklimburg.voka.be

"This is a book that is a must for anyone who is serious about networking. If you do it, it will save you years in building your network. Remember the best way to increase your net worth is to increase your network."

***Nigel Risner***, International Speaker and author of *"You Had Me at Hello,"* www.nigelrisner.com

"Jan clearly has a strong understanding of the role of networking for the modern businessman and how to network effectively. This book is clearly written and is an important tool for people that are new to the networking scene and for people who consider themselves to be experts."

***Andy Lopata***, Managing Director, BRE Networking, www.brenet.co.uk

## What others say about *"Let's Connect!"*

"When asked to review his latest accomplishment, I found it hard to separate the book from the man. Jan Vermeiren is one of those people that genuinely live the story that they tell. For me such integrity is highly stimulating. It demonstrates that in life you can make things happen. It shows that doing what is best all things considered really does make things right – in whatever direction you choose to go. In this book Jan shares his extensive expertise in networking. He is not only thorough in terms of what to do; he also gives easy-to-execute suggestions on how to do it. This mix of theory and practice will immediately launch you into effective networking, as it did for me. Very powerful indeed!"

***Cees J. de Bruin***, Business Facilitator, www.notthecarrot.com

"Jan is THE networking expert. What I most admire about Jan is his drive, his knowledge about networking and most of all, the example he sets. If you want to know what networking in action means, just observe him for some time and you will know what I mean."

***Wim Van Acker***, Coaching for Clarity in Your Business, www.wimvanacker. com

***""Let's Connect!"*** is a remarkable and most exhaustive guide for anyone attempting to create a productive, satisfying network. But most of all it demonstrates that networking is different from selling, that it is a natural process of building long-lasting relationships, using your own style and personality, based on a universal law of "giving before receiving.""

***Greet Pipijn***, founder Emotionele Intelligentie Instituut, www.emotioneleintelligentie.be

"Jan Vermeiren's networking book is a solid addition to the growing number of books on the subject."

***Melissa Giovagnoli***, President of Networlding, Author of Networlding, www.networlding.com

# Let's Connect!

"Jan Vermeiren eats, drinks, sleeps and breathes networking. His passion in life is inspiring people to become better networkers and in making then more successful in life. Jan is a giver, always on the lookout to help and support people around him. That's his secret to success. With his book, *"Let's Connect!"* he is now sharing his networking intelligence with all of us. Read it, digest it and use it! This is your ticket to success. Let Jan be your Networking Coach!"

***Hendrik Deckers***, Chairman Ecademy Benelux (benelux.ecademy.com) and Founder CIOnet (www.cionet.com)

"Before I read this book I had no positive thoughts and feelings about networking. Jan Vermeiren, "The Networking Coach" gave me another idea about the matter. Networking is something else than sales blah blah. His clear theories and personal storytelling style turned networking into a major added value in my life and those around me. Sharing is growing!"

***Jan De Boeck,*** The SPEAK coach, www.improvementforyou.be

"Networking is a new art and skill and a lot of people are starting to wake up to the fact realizing that it is no longer an option but an essential skill. The problem is where and who to turn to in order to learn this vital skill? Secondary schools, universities and business schools don't even touch on it, let alone study it in depth.

Time spent with a master lecturer called Jan Vermeiren on how to network effectively will give you clarity to you in a way that illuminates the path and mental approach that is so necessary for success in this crucial activity. In addition to his obvious knowledge, it is as much his manner and nature that convinces you that this is a man worth listening to who offers a wealth of experience and simple practical steps to ensure that your networking activities bring about the results you seek."

***Andrew Widgery***, Ecademy Global and UK Development Manager, www.ecademy.com

## What others say about *"Let's Connect!"*

*""Let's Connect!"* hits the core of networking head on. A very insightful, informative, practical and easy read. This book is a must for anyone interested in boosting their networking skills. Read it, enjoy it and learn from it. I will make sure my friends read this book!"

***Bert Verdonck***, Managing Director Bioptimo, www.bioptimo.com

"This book renewed my awareness about what a process networking is. Every step in the process is important. Jan proves yet again that if you work at networking it will work for you."

***Carl Van Dyck***, Director VKW Antwerpen-Mechelen, www.vkw.be

"Very easy to put into practice, very smooth reading, to-the-point practical guide for anyone wanting to polish up their networking skills. The alternation of (not too dry) theory, with practical examples and concrete tips, kept me captivated as a reader. I felt that what I learned can be broadly applied to a wide range of different contacts with other people."

***Hilde Van Damme***, Coordinator UNIZO-startersservice, www.unizo.be

"Great book packed with valuable information for anyone interested in enhancing their ability to connect with others. I really like *"Let's Connect!"* because it is an enjoyable read, the information is organized well, there are interesting examples and it is important information."

***Donna Fisher***, Author of *Power Networking and Professional Networking for Dummies,* www.donnafisher.com

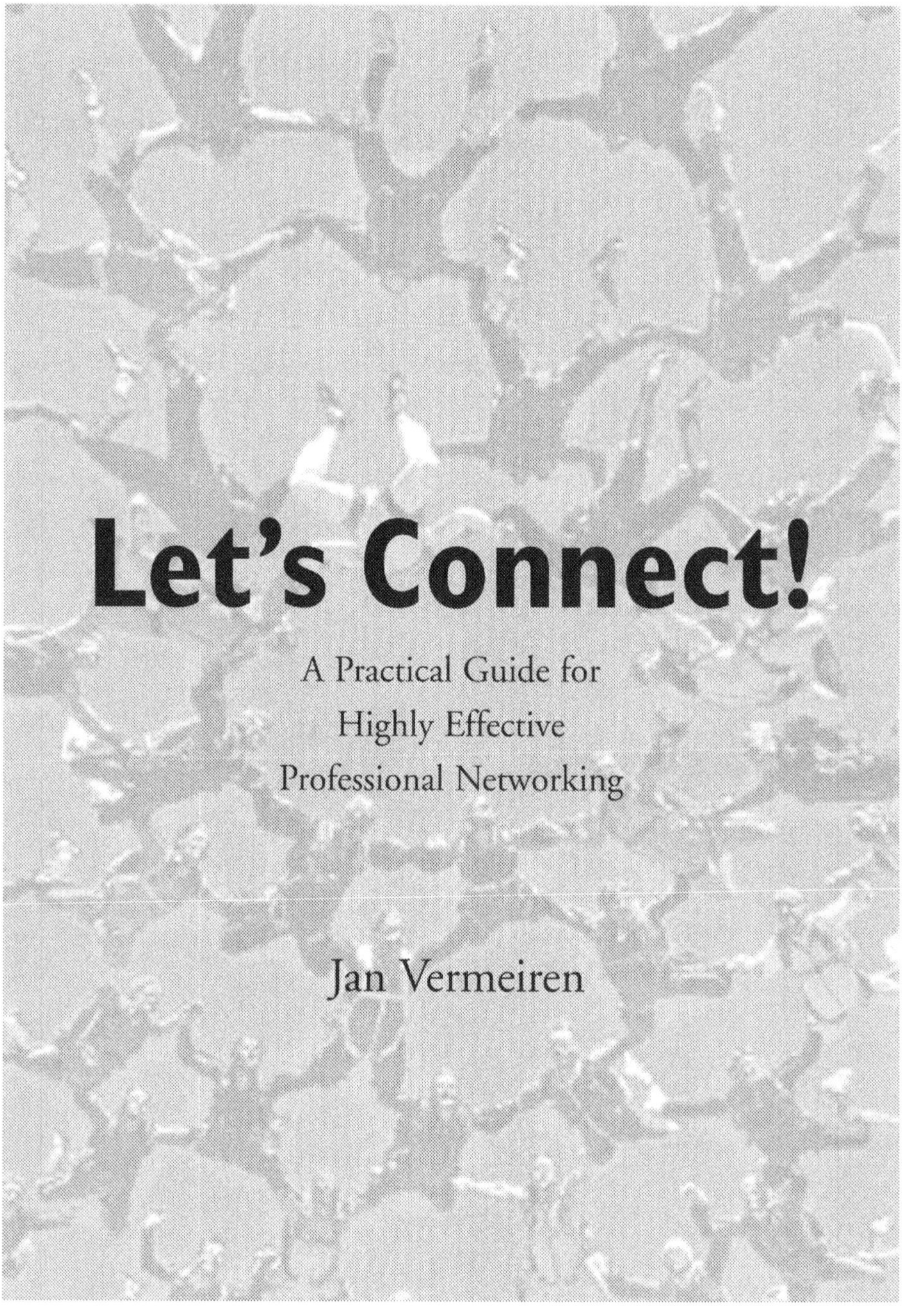

# Let's Connect!

## A Practical Guide for Highly Effective Professional Networking

Jan Vermeiren

M·J

New York

To my network, which was, is and ever will be the catalyst of my inspiration, success and happiness.

**Let's Connect!**



Paperback ISBN: 978-1-60037-261-2
eBook ISBN: 978-1-60037-262-9

Published by:

MORGAN · JAMES
THE ENTREPRENEURIAL PUBLISHER
www.morganjamespublishing.com

Habitat for Humanity®
Peninsula Building Partner

1225 Franklin Avenue Suite 325
Garden Citry, NY 11530-1693
800-485-4943
www.MorganJamesPublishing.com
Info@MorganJamesPublishing.com

Cover design by:
Heather Kirk
Heather@DesignsByHeather.com
Interior Design By:
Bill James
Bill@WAJames.com

Printed in the United States of America

# Short table of contents

# Table of contents

## Table of contents

Table of contents

# Foreword: Networking: old wine in new bags?

Are you tired of hearing the word "networking" over and over again? Everybody tells you about the importance of networking, but you feel that you have something else/better to do? Or do you think that networking is only for the in-crowd and not for you? Maybe you don't feel comfortable attending networking events and you recognize Geert Conard's situation (from his book, *"A Girlfriend in Every City"*):

*"I was always horrified when I had to walk into a room full of strangers by myself...and had to try and make conversation with whoever seemed up for it...often I just stood at the side and watched the crowd."*

If you're thinking, "This is exactly my situation," then this book definitely has your name on it. If you are already comfortable with networking at an event, then you might benefit from the very practical tips and networking secrets that are revealed in this book to network more efficiently, more effectively and with more fun.

I wrote this book because of the tremendous value of networking. There is value for everyone, not just for sales people like in most books about networking. In an ever rapidly changing world, it is good to have a safety net: your network.

The importance of networking is incessantly increasing. In their book, "Funky Business," Kjell Nordstrom and Jonas Ridderstrale define today's society as follows: *"The "surplus" society has a surplus of similar companies, employing similar people, with similar educational backgrounds, working in similar jobs, coming up with similar ideas, producing similar things, with similar prices and similar quality."*

How are you going to make a difference? As a company you could possibly solve this by adapting your marketing strategy. What can you do as a salesperson or as an employee if you don't have any impact on the marketing strategy? Where do you find the time (and expertise) if you are a small business owner or freelancer?

There is good news. You really can make a difference. In the first place by providing high quality service to your network (inside and outside your company). Secondly, by tapping into the power of networking.

Not only is networking becoming more important, it has always been and will always be a very effective and cheap way to move on in life. In her book, "Professional Networking for Dummies," Donna Fisher writes that in the USA more than 70% of the people find a new job via their network. Networking cuts both ways: recruiters also use their network to speed up the process of finding the right candidates. They use their network as a preliminary filter so they don't have to review hundreds of resumes. Also, in the USA, the Bristol Business School found that 70% of the revenues of small business owners come from their network.

In a more private atmosphere networking helps you to find a cozy restaurant, a relaxing movie, an inspirational book, a reliable baby sitter, a friendly dentist and maybe even your dream house.

Networking becomes more important and is an easy and fun way to get things done. But how do you do it? Where do you start? How do you behave?

We were never taught networking at school or any other place. Like many other important things in life like discovering your passion and handling money, networking is apparently a skill we are supposed to learn by ourselves. That's not always easy; so let this book be your guide on the networking path.

There are lots of good books about networking on the market. You can find a number of them at the back of the book and on my website. I learned a lot from the books and from the people who wrote them. You can see this book partly as my way of thanking and honoring them. Next to the insights I got from them, I also want to thank the participants of my networking training courses for telling me their stories and experiences. I learned a lot from them as well. This brings me to the intention with which I wrote this book:

*To give you a solid foundation and insight in the dynamics of networking combined with some very practical tips for networking at events and on the Web no matter what your current professional or personal situation.*

Networking is important in every stage of life and in every aspect. However, this book focuses primarily on how to network in a business environment. Not only in sales, but also as a way to interact with colleagues, customers, suppliers, partners and all other involved parties.

Maybe you are very eager to go to the practical tips right away. However, to better understand the tips, I recommend that you read the book in the sequence it is presented to you. You'll gain insights in the foundations and the attitude of networking. If you know them, it is easy to find the right approach and tools yourself. Remember the story of the three little pigs: the wolf blew the houses of the pigs that didn't have a foundation away in no time. Don't allow this to happen to your networking efforts!

Enjoy!

Jan

## Some important notes about the book:

- *Because I believe in men and women being equal, I will sometimes use the word "he" and sometimes "she" when I mean "a person of any gender."*
- *Sometimes, I use a word that might not be familiar to you. At the back of the book there is a "used terms" section where these words are explained.*

- *In the first chapter you'll find an overview of "Frequently Asked Networking Questions" with references to the parts of the book that contain the answer. You can always come back to this chapter to find a quick answer to a specific question.*
- *A good way to get the most out of this book is:*

  1. *Read it once so you understand the fundamentals and dynamics of networking.*
  2. *Choose one or more concepts, ideas or tips that appeal to you and then commit yourself to bringing them into practice. Don't go for all of them at once. Just do it step by step!*
  3. *Reread the book a few months later and choose other concepts that appeal to you. By practicing the first ones you chose, you will already notice some changes in your life. Other tips that you might have "missed" the first time will become more relevant the second time around.*

***Networking tip:*** if you feel uncomfortable putting some of these tips into practice, especially when other people are involved, you can always use this sentence: "I just read a book about networking where the advice was to..." Not only will people be more susceptible to what you are going to say, they will also be interested in hearing other tips. This way you can share what you have learned, be of service and start to build a relationship with them!

# FANQ (Frequently Asked Networking Questions)

In my work as the Networking Coach I'm confronted with lots of questions about networking. In this book you will find a compilation of my answers. To give you an idea about what you can expect from this book, you are presented with the most frequently asked questions and the reference to the part(s) and page(s) where you can find an answer to these questions:

- ***What is networking?*** See: page 21
- ***Why is networking becoming increasingly important?*** See: page 11
- Which ***mental barriers*** to networking are there? See: page 23
- What is the ***networking attitude?*** See: page 23
- What has ***passion*** to do with networking? See: page 31
- Why are my ***values*** important in networking? See: page 32
- Why set ***goals*** in networking? See: page 34
- What is a ***good goal?*** See: page 34
- How do I tap into the power of ***my network to reach my goals faster?*** See: page 38
- How do I approach the ***best people for my network?*** See: page 42
- What are the ***6 degrees of proximity?*** See: page 45
- ***Is it really a small world?*** See: page 45
- What is the ***difference between networking and (hard) selling?*** See: page 54

## Let's Connect!

## FANQ

## Let's Connect!

## FANQ

- ***Which follow-up actions can I do?*** See: page 215
- What is the ***difference between an introduction and a referral?*** See: page 219
- How do I ***introduce two people via email?*** See: page 222
- ***When do I write an introduction and when a referral email?*** See: page 228
- ***What do I do when somebody I don't know very well asks for an introduction?*** See: page 231
- How do I ***ask for a referral or introduction***? See: page 234
- ***When to use which communication medium?*** See: page 234

Now you know what to expect in this book. So now it is time to start with the basics, the foundation of networking.

# Chapter 1

# The Foundation Of Your Network

How did you find your last home? Where did you book your last vacation? In which restaurant did you last eat? If you're involved in sales: what's the percentage of new or recurring sales you get from word-of-mouth?

Most of the time, you got the information or the sales leads via someone you already knew or via someone from your network.

But what is networking really? How do you start? Where do you begin?

In this chapter you gain more insights in the dynamics behind networking. We also look at how to lay a solid foundation for your networking actions. An insight in the dynamics of networking will help you to network more effectively, efficiently and with more fun. Moreover, it will help you to put potential disappointments (arrogant people, unreturned calls or time wasters) in the right perspective and keep confidence. Networking works!

## Networking: what is it and what is it not

Networking. This is typically one of those words where you get one hundred different definitions from one hundred different people. At least that is more or less what I experience in my training courses. Everybody can imagine what it means, but nobody really knows. Networking is basically one of those words that have almost as many interpretations as there are people on the face of the earth.

In the Merriam-Webster dictionary "networking" is described as: "the exchange of information or services among individuals, groups, or institutions."

It's a start, but for me it's only part of the truth. The reason why I use it nonetheless, is because it's concise and because it disregards the aspect of "selling" or "taking." These latter words make "networking" sound negative for many people while it such a positive word!

With this in mind let's explore the different meanings of the word "networking."

Depending on the context, networking can be viewed from different angles:

- The networking activity
- The networking attitude
- The networking process
- Networking as an organizational driver or barrier

In this book the focus is on the attitude and necessary skills to be successful in the process and on networking activities. Networking as an organizational driver or barrier will not be covered. An excellent book about this topic is, "The Hidden Powers of Social Networks" by Rob Cross and Andrew Parker.

## The activity

"Networking" is generally used to describe all the steps you undertake at a reception or another event where people gather in a professional environment. This is, however, only the tip of the iceberg. Networking is also about helping each other out in a personal environment. Helping somebody to move to a new apartment, recommending a nice restaurant or lending your car to your brother are a few examples how we can constantly network in our daily lives.

If we go back to the statement that "Networking" is generally used to describe all the steps you undertake at a professional event, we get to something that many people fear in one way or the other. How do you feel when somebody says, "let's go networking" or if your boss orders you to "go networking?" Are you looking forward to it? Or do you feel the stress already?

Many people have questions like: "What do I have to say? With whom should I talk? Will I know anyone? What if they don't like me or don't want to talk to me? Won't they perceive me as "too pushy" or, just the opposite, too timid? How long do I have to talk to someone? Will there be someone I can enter the room with so I won't be alone from the beginning? What if this person wants to stay with me all the time? Wouldn't this jeopardize my chances of getting to know other people? What if people remember me, but I can't remember THEIR names? How can I use the Internet to help me in my networking efforts?"

Do you have one or more of these questions? If so, you will certainly benefit from the tips in this book. As a matter of fact, most of this book is about networking action, about networking as an activity.

## The attitude

Before you start (or continue) networking, be aware that your attitude towards networking determines the degree of your "success." Your attitude is your foundation. However, only a few people are aware of their attitude towards networking. What about you? Are you aware of how you feel about networking?

Throughout her book "People Power", networking guru Donna Fisher points out several mental barriers to networking. Most people don't realize they have them. Carefully read the list. If you recognize any of the following thinking patterns, you might find that they limit your networking abilities:

- They probably don't have time to...
- They wouldn't want to...
- I don't need anyone's help

- I can do this by myself
- I know what needs to be done here
- I don't want to bother people
- I can't call her: she's too busy
- I don't know them well enough to call them
- People will think I'm weak/needy/stupid if I approach them about this
- I should be smart enough to figure this out by myself
- I have no right to expect others to help me out
- They probably don't know anyone who could help me
- I don't want them to realize I need help with this
- I don't want them to know I don't know how to handle this

Where do these inhibitions come from?

In life, we are conditioned by the culture we live in and by the people who surround us. In our early years we can't choose; our parents choose for us. Mostly without doing it intentionally, next to positive values and beliefs, they pass on certain values or beliefs that prohibit you, me and many other people from networking optimally.

Still according to Fisher there are seven types of conditioning that can influence your networking effectiveness without you even realizing it. This is an overview of these seven types, complete with a reference to the chapter where you can find the solution:

| Type | Comments |
|---|---|
| **"Don't talk to strangers"** | This is wise advice for a small child who doesn't know how to make the distinction between right and wrong. However, as an adult, the situation is different. Talking to people you haven't met before opens the doors to a wide variety of opportunities (see the tips about "Making contact" on page 141). |

| Type | Comments |
|---|---|
| **"Be strong"** | Some people think being strong means not asking for help, doing everything on their own and being other people's savior or hero. "Being strong" really means knowing what you want and asking others to help you reach your goals (see the tips about "Goals" on page 34). |
| **"Be a big boy" or "Be a big girl"** | Too many people confuse being childlike (being playful and joyful) with being childish. The enthusiasm of a child is a great character trait at any age! (see the tips about "Passion" on page 31) |
| **"You can't trust others"** | Most of us have one or more negative experiences with misplaced trust. This may have been very painful and it can also be the reason for never trusting anyone again. However, a life of not trusting is not much of a life. Learn to bring people who are worthy of your trust in your network and be trustworthy yourself (see the tips about "Trust" on page 88). |
| **"Don't bother that person"** | If you were ever told not to bother people, this thought may have been internalized as "You are a bother" or "What you want is not important" or "Others are more important." This internal belief could prohibit you unconsciously to contact others, but you are not a bother. People are only a bother when they are selfish or inappropriate with their words, timing, actions or behaviors. It's OK to call people. People want to contribute, especially when you can call on them in such a way that they feel acknowledged and included. They will be happy to help you (see "The best question in networking" on page 77) |
| **"Don't depend on others"** | If you heard this as a child, this probably came from the mouth of someone who had a painful encounter with misplaced trust. However, it is good advice if it means that you should take your life in your own hands instead of depending on parents, a partner or Social Security. You don't have to fully rely on others. I encourage you to have an interdependent attitude. Look for ways you can help others and how they can help you (see also the tips about "The Golden Triangle of networking" on page 63). |

| Type | Comments |
|---|---|
| **"Don't let yourself be hurt"** | This is probably the reaction of someone who has been hurt by someone else and is reluctant to trust other people. No matter what you do, you can't protect yourself from ever getting hurt, disappointed or misunderstood again. When you give with no strings attached, without conditions and without expecting anything in return, you cannot be "used." You run the risk of feeling used when you give more than you can afford to give (financially, mentally or emotionally) and you expect or even need something in return. Give only what you can afford to give and feel good about giving (see also the tips about "Giving" on page 64). |

## The most important networking attitude

For me there is one attitude in networking that is of the utmost importance. It is the very foundation of networking. I call it the "Give and Receive" attitude. This is the definition:

> ***"Sharing information in a proactive and reactive way without expecting anything in return."***

Let's have a more detailed look at this definition:

- **Information:** in this definition "information" refers to both very general and very specific knowledge. For example, how do you record a television program with a video recorder? Or what is the specific code of the newest software programming language? "Information" is also about business issues, like sales leads, and about simple day-to-day stuff (like "what are the opening hours of the supermarket"). In a professional environment, "information" is, for example, a job opening, sales lead, a new supplier or employee, opportunities for partnerships, interesting training courses or tips to work more efficiently.

- **Sharing:** this involves two parties. Networking is not a one-way street, but a two or more way boulevard. It is always about a win-win situation, in which all parties are satisfied. What's important in this concept is that you are comfortable with making requests and being open for help and being willing to accept this help yourself.

- **In a proactive and reactive way:** in the first place this means that you offer information or help when you are asked to do so (reactive), but it goes further than that. You can send people information and refer them to others, without them asking to do this (proactive). Make sure you don't SPAM them. A good approach could be to let them know you have this information and that you are willing to share it, especially, when you don't know people well. This might be a non-confrontational approach.

- **Without expecting anything in return:** in this era of short term benefits it's not a concept that's immediately embraced by everybody. It is the one that works best in the long run, and it builds trust and makes you more "attractive" to other people.

By giving without expecting anything back, you will eventually receive much more than your initial "investment," but you never know from whom or when. That's something many people have difficulty with. In my training courses this is always the start of a lively discussion because only a few people see how they can realize this without investing lots of time and money. In the tip about "The Golden Triangle of networking" (on page 63) you get some examples of how to give without expecting anything in return and also without having to "regret" this later on.

Remember that networking is a **long-term** game that **always involves two or more players.** You reap what you've sown. Start sowing (sharing) so you can reap more and faster!

## The process

If you really want to tap into the powers of networking, a proactive attitude is highly recommended. Together with Hendrik Deckers (you can read his blog at www.hendrikdeckers.com) I came up with the following definition of the proactive networking process:

**"Proactive networking is the systematic, planned and prepared process of managing your existing connections and establishing relationships with new people so that all parties can tap into their network to reach personal and professional objectives."**

It's a rather long definition, but we feel that it contains all the necessary elements to define successful networking:

- **Process:** networking is not about attending one meeting or contacting the people from your network only when you need them. It's like in physics: it costs lots of energy to get a body into motion, but when it's moving, the required amount of energy is much lower. Keeping in touch costs less energy than your initial "investment" in meeting new people. The real pay offs are in the long run.
- **Systematic, planned and prepared:** planning and preparing increases your effectiveness (doing the right things) and efficiency (doing the things right). Especially when you still have the idea that networking only costs time, it will benefit you to plan and prepare your networking efforts.
- **Managing existing connections:** trying to expand your network is one thing, preserving your existing one is another. Often it's more beneficial to maintain your current contacts and 27 deepen your relationship with them as opposed to hunting for new ones. To be efficient and effective at managing your current connections, tools like email software and online networks are very useful. You get tips about those tools in the chapter on online networking (see page 183).

- **Establishing relationships with new people:** everything in life is changing at an ever-faster pace. This applies to you and your network, too. New situations, challenges and opportunities in life call for other people. The people you were close to in primary school probably don't belong to your closest circle of friends anymore. Make sure that you are always on the lookout for new connections, but also beware that you don't lose contact with your current network.
- **All parties:** as already mentioned, networking is a two way street. Give and ye shall receive!
- **Personal and professional:** networking is often viewed from a professional point of view, but also in your personal life, networking has great value. Remember the last time you needed a plumber? I guess you were happy that you had one in your network or that somebody referred you to one. Or maybe you wished that you had networked more proactively in the past because you could not find (a good) one?
- **Objectives:** this relates to the systematic, planned and prepared character of the process. Your network is a free and very powerful aid to reach your goals. You can read more about them in the next chapter about goals.

Having the mentality of a proactive networker will allow you to tap into the power of your network more easily, efficiently and effectively. There are other, more fundamental things that will determine your level of success in networking: your passion, values and goals.

## Passion, Values and Goals

For the largest part of my life, I felt like I was living on a group of islands. Unfortunately, I don't mean a vacation under palm trees. Like a group of islands, all parts of my life were closely related to each other, but not really connected. It cost me energy to "travel" between my "islands:" family, school, basketball club, and different groups of friends...I felt that on every island only one aspect of myself could display itself, but that nobody got to see the whole picture, including myself. A few years ago I realized that the reason was that I never took the time to think about my passion, values or goals. And because no one ever asked me.

about my passion, values or goals or taught me about them at school, I thought it was normal to have to play a different role in every other situation. Now I can tell you: this is not normal. Once I had discovered this for myself, I talked about it with other people. Most of them told me that they didn't really think about it and "just lived their life." What about you? Have you thought about it?

I was also doing things on my own. I never needed help from anybody. I still have this tendency from time to time, when writing this book, for example, but I also experienced that living a life, surrounded by a fantastic group of people is not only easier, but also more rewarding. At the very moment that I'm writing this, my landlord is going to the "container park" (where they recycle stuff and process garbage) for me as a "thank you" for bringing him and his wife to the airport for their vacation a few weeks ago. It is nice to experience the support of other people.

Another example is from my business: I absolutely dislike cold calling. After being in business for a few years, my network works for me and introduces and refers me to new customers and business partners, and I don't have to cold call anymore. I do the same for them, I refer them to other people I meet. I feel very grateful being the receiver as well as being the giver. Isn't it nice to experience this abundance in business?

Why do we tend to refer some people more often than others? One of the reasons is that we trust one person more than another. Another, and in many cases, an even more important factor is that people with a compelling passion, strong values and clear goals appeal a lot to other people. Such people are valued more highly because they have a drive to make things happen for them and their network. In order to increase your value to your network, and the value of your network to you, it is primordial to know your passion, values and goals.

However, you can choose not to think about your passion, values and goals and still networking will work for you. But why limit yourself? Why shouldn't you go for more, reach for the sky, go for what you deserve? The only reason I can think of is that you did not really know how to go about it. In the next paragraphs you will find tips and websites that will get you started in the right direction. At the end of the book, you'll find a value discovery exercise that might also be helpful. Finding out what your values are is only a small investment of your time, but your personal and professional life will look very different as a result of it.

## Passion

You read that one of the breakthroughs in my life was finding my passion, values and goals. What makes finding one's passion so important?

There are many reasons, but a very simple and practical one is this. By knowing your passion, you get more energy to do:

- What you want to do
- What you "have" to do

Knowing your passion will give you energy instead of taking it away from you. You will reach your goals faster and easier. When living your passion, you get more opportunities to get into "flow." In "flow" everything runs smoother and you really enjoy doing the things you are doing, even if it is physically tough. In his book, "Flow," Mihaly Csikszentmihalyi gives many examples of chess players and mountain climbers who forgot their mental or physical "pain" once they were in flow.

Another advantage of knowing your passion and being able to live in your passion for several hours a day, is that the things that you enjoy less, become less of a burden. Filling in papers, doing administrative work, cleaning, washing, ironing...are not on the top of most people's favorite "to do list," but if you have found your passion, you take on these tasks with a smile.

Now is the big question: how do you find your passion? Where motivation and excellence meet, that's where you find passion. You'll know a job, task or project is a passion when it's easy, fun and time slips away because you are totally engaged. For me, it's when I train people in networking – when I coach them, when I write about it, when I connect people with each other, when I talk about networking. Now you know my passion, can you tell me what YOUR passion is? If not, this might be a good time to think about it.

When you find your passion, it is good to share this with other people. They will experience you as being more enthusiastic. If you really found your passion, you will radiate this. You will speak in a very moving way, there are sparks in your eyes and you are literally "full of your subject." People will notice this not only on a conscious, but also on a subconscious level. As a consequence, they will be more "attracted" to you. Another advantage is that more of the "right" people will notice you. These are the people who can benefit from what you do with your passion.

The outcome of knowing your passion and radiating it is more and better help from your network. This in turn, will help your network grow by attracting the right people.

To find your passion, it helps a lot to get more insight into yourself. On the Internet there are several websites that offer free tests to get you on the way. You can visit, for example, Queendom (www.queendom.com), Tickle (www.tickle.com) or All the tests (www.allthetests.com). In our training courses we use a variant of the DISC profiling system that we developed together with Carol Dysart. You can get your full DISC profile at her website: www.caroldysart.com

## Values

What do you find important in life? What are your values?

Not many people have really given thought to this question despite its importance. Values are the principles that guide your actions on a daily basis. Living your professional and personal life according to those values creates a sense of authenticity in the way you present yourself. Authenticity inspires trust and confidence. These are most probably the most important values in networking.

Most of the people that did give thought to their values are glad they did. They are aware that decisions that are aligned with those values give them more satisfaction, and they are also aware that other people might have different values and, as a consequence, won't make the same decisions. For many of them it stops with this awareness. They don't find a way to apply their values in practice.

By knowing your values, you will have the criteria to check if a specific task or project will give you satisfaction and joy. They can also be the criteria to decide whether or not something is right for you. Sometimes it's better to delegate a task or project to somebody else. If it's not aligned with your values, but with those of a colleague, then you're better off passing on the job.

Here's an example: Let's say that one of your values is "involvement." You get a project that involves joining forces with someone you really don't like. Chances are that you are going to postpone all tasks concerning this project because you dislike this person, and then you start feeling bad about the project. You get this feeling because your heart is not into it. A solution might be to team up with someone else. Or to "loosen" the cooperation or communicate via a third party like a project leader you are more comfortable with.

If you don't know your values yet, you can do the value discovery exercise at the end of the book (see page 241).

By sharing your values, you (and others) will also have the criteria to check if cooperating with somebody else will be easy or difficult. This applies to your professional life, be it as a member of a team, a partnership between organizations or a customer-supplier relationship, and to your personal life.

If we look back to the example, another solution might be found in the sharing of your values. Maybe you'll find out that you share other values, like "being result oriented" or "family." You can relate to the other person on the basis of other values than "involvement." Or maybe she didn't know about your rather negative feelings towards her and you discover that this was based on a misunderstanding. Sharing and talking about values creates a very open atmosphere, which is the basis for a solution (instead of problem) oriented approach.

In order to understand and help each other better it is good to talk about your values and to know the values of others.

*"It's all about relationships. When you connect with great people who have similar core values where you consciously collaborate, you live your life at a whole new level – a level where you can create incredible opportunities daily." (Melissa Giovagnoli in Networlding).*

## Goals

You've probably heard of the power of goal setting. At least I hope so. But have you put this knowledge to good use? Do you set goals on a regular basis?

Most people haven't heard about goal setting or don't practice it. However, people who set goals are far more successful than others. Studies at the universities of Harvard and Stanford show that only 15% of the students have goals. Only 3% write them down. When the researchers contacted those students 20 years later, they discovered that the 15% who had goals were on average financially doing twice as well as the other 85%. The 3% with written goals even did 10 times better than the other 97%.

I hope the results of these studies inspire you to pay more attention to your goals. In networking they will be of great value to you.

By knowing your goals, you will be more focused and have something to work towards. Your goals are also criteria that can help you decide whether to spend your time on a particular task or opportunity or not. They can help you decide which networking events to attend and which not.

The power of (written) goal setting is this: when you identify the goals that are most important to you, you consciously and subconsciously begin to figure out ways you can make them come true. You develop the attitudes, abilities, skills, and financial capacity to reach them. You begin seeing previously overlooked opportunities to bring yourself closer to the achievement of your goals.

You can attain almost any goal you set when you plan your steps wisely and establish a time frame that allows you to carry out those steps. Goals that may have seemed far away and out of reach eventually move closer and become feasible, not because your goals shrink, but because you grow and expand to match them. When you list your goals you build your self-image. You see yourself worthy of these goals, and develop the traits and personality that allow you to reach them. When your self-confidence grows, your fears to contact other people will disappear. As a consequence you will feel more comfortable at networking events.

What are the characteristics of good goals? As you probably have heard in many courses, goals have to be S.M.A.R.T. This is an acronym for:

- Specific
- Measurable
- Attainable/Acceptable
- Realistic
- Timely

Let's dig deeper into the SMART definition. Why? Because this is the fundament of reaching every goal. Making things SMART and acting upon it, is what makes the difference – not only for the 3% at Stanford and Harvard, but also in your life!

| Type | Comments |
| --- | --- |
| **Specific** | A specific goal has a much greater chance of being accomplished than a general goal.<br>*Example: a general goal would be: "Get in shape." A specific goal would look like this: "Join a health club and workout three days a week."* |
| **Measurable** | Make sure you have concrete criteria for measuring progress toward the attainment of each goal you set. There is a saying "If you can't measure it, you can't manage it." Measuring the progress means that you set milestones and intermediary deadlines.<br>*Example: "I want to have $100,000 in my savings account before I turn 35" might be a good and measurable goal. "I want to save some money" is not as measurable.* |
| **Attainable / Acceptable** | You probably won't commit to working on goals, which are too far out of your reach. On the other hand a goal needs to stretch you slightly. This way you feel you can do it, while making a real commitment. When you achieve what you set out to do, the feeling of success will help you stay motivated. Your goal should also be set by you rather than by someone else.<br>*Example: if you aim to lose 20 pounds in one week, we all know that isn't achievable. But when you set a goal to lose one pound and achieve this, you will be motivated to lose the next pound.* |
| **Realistic** | To be realistic, a goal must represent an objective toward which you are both willing and able to work. A goal can be both high and realistic; you are the only one who can decide just how high your goal should be. Be sure that every goal represents substantial progress. A high goal is often easier to reach than a low one because a low goal exerts low motivational force.<br>*Example: it may be more realistic to set a goal of eating a piece of fruit each day instead of one sweet item than banning all sweets out of your life. You can then choose to work towards* |

| Type | Comments |
|---|---|
| Realistic | *reducing the amount of sweet products gradually as and when this feels realistic for you.*<br><br>Realistic also means that you can do it without having to sacrifice (too much of) sleep, family, social life, work or other important aspects of your life. |
| Timely | "Timely" has two components:<br><br>1. What are the milestones and (small and large) deadlines?<br><br>2. When are you going to do it?<br><br>Set a time frame for your goal: for next week, in three months, by the end of the semester. Putting a deadline on your goal gives you a ***clear target*** to work towards.<br><br>If you don't set a time, the commitment is too vague. It tends not to happen because you feel you can start at any time. Without a time limit, there's no urgency to start taking action now.<br><br>Write down when you plan to work on your goal, for example, between 4:00 - 5:00 p.m. Another tip: anything that will take you more than two hours to complete, should be broken into smaller, more manageable chunks. |

## What about your goals?

I hear over and over again in my training courses and workshops: "We already know SMART," but when I ask the participants what they do with this knowledge, most of them remain silent. What about you? Did you do something with this knowledge? Are you reaching your goals? No? Revise them and see if they are really SMART. If they are, share them with your network. If they are not SMART, also share them with your network. They can help you to get them SMART.

***Brian Tracy: Goals in writing are dreams with deadlines.***

## Reach your goals by sharing them with your network

By sharing your goals, you will receive help from others to reach them. If people feel that you want to reach your goals and do the things you do with passion and live by your values, they will be very likely to help.

Remember the last time your little nephew told you about his favorite sport (let's say tennis), with little sparks of energy in his eyes? He told you vividly about how he saw himself in fifteen years, as the new world number one – the new Pete Sampras, John McEnroe or Roger Federer. He could see himself a great champion at Wimbledon with people screaming his name and applauding him. Then he told you that in order to raise some more money to buy the necessary gear he was washing cars. By doing this, he was taking his first step to his personal success. Did you ever consider for a second telling him that you just went to the car wash three days ago? If you're like 98% of the human population on this earth you've already opened your purse and you're happy to contribute to fulfilling his dream.

When I had set the goal of writing this book and told my network about it, they came up with suggestions for the content. They also offered to bring me in contact with publishers and to proofread this book. It felt great to have this support. The people from your network can do similar things for you. Just share your goals with them!

One of the reviewers of the book asked me why I didn't give an example of a goal with respect to networking like expanding your network with 50 new people in the coming three months. I asked him: "What would you do with these 50 people?" "Then I would always have someone to call for information about the rapidly changing legal aspects in my sector. Lots of money can be lost or gained with this information," he answered. I replied: "Then your real goal is probably: Be able to have an answer on a legal topic within 24 hours." A "sub goal" could then be expanding your network with 50 well chosen people. Expanding or maintaining your network is not a goal itself, but it could be part of a larger goal. It is very important to have this larger goal clear first before doing any actions or making any sub goals.

## Your network as the best aid to reach your goals

"The person who can help me best to reach my goal, sleeps next to me!" was a remark of Joris van Rooy (Sales Manager Northern Europe, Nike) in one of my "Smart Networking" workshops.

His comment may surprise you, but not me. When we think of someone to help us solve a problem or reach a goal, we tend to think of the same people over and over again. The ones we see as very knowledgeable. They helped us in one area and then in a second, and suddenly they became the overall experts. On the other hand, there is the danger of only thinking in terms of specialists. We see them as a specialist in one area, but never take the effort to discover other specialties or interests they might have.

The most common "mistake" in both cases is that we only look at what value they can add personally. We tend to forget that they have a network of interesting, competent and inspiring people, too. The latter is what happened to Joris. He had forgotten that his wife knew people who could help him reach his goal.

In one of the exercises in my training courses, we focus on "the people who are in the best position" to help you reach your goal. The most common "mistake" participants make is that they interpret this assignment as "the people who are in the best position AND ALREADY BELONG TO MY NETWORK." They already limit themselves to their own network of (on average) 250 people.

> ***Networking success tip: make a list of the people that are best placed to help you reach your goal, even if they don't belong to your network (yet).***

If you free yourself of this way of thinking and list the "best people," then you already took a big step towards reaching your goal. The second step will then be to reach those best-placed people via your network or your network's network. If the "best people" are still "a bridge too far," then you can "downgrade" to "second best." The most important thing about this exercise is that you begin from the best possible situation. This is something only a few of us do. Why? Because we never learned it!

Now back to the example of Joris. What happened was that he wrote down the name of the person that could best help him and then he realized that his wife could bring him in contact with this person.

So, the first group of people to think about is the people that are placed best, even if they don't belong to your network.

A second group of important, but often-neglected people to help you reach your goals is mentors and coaches. They are your indirect support. They don't necessarily help you reach a specific goal, but they guide you on your way.

For me the most important thing is the skill of a mentor or coach to ask good questions. Most things in life we know ourselves, but we don't realize it. We get so many inputs throughout the day and it is not always easy to distinguish the things that are important for us from matters that are not that relevant. When a coach asks the right questions, you don't only find the answers, but you also realize you had them in you. This is much more powerful than listening to an expert, reading a book or doing what somebody else tells you to do.

Do you have a mentor or a coach? This doesn't have to be expensive. You can hire one, but you can also ask a neighbor or a family member to be your mentor. There are mentoring programs in many organizations. Did you already check if there is one in your organization, too? If not, what holds you back from starting one yourself?

What Robbins suggests is that you make sure that in every area of your life, personal and professional, there is a core group of people with higher standards and expectations than your own. They will lift you up, inspire you, stimulate you, challenge you and ensure you will reach your goals. Does this sound strange to you? Think about this: if you are a tennis player and you want to improve, who do you play with: opponents that are weaker or stronger than you? From whom do you learn the most?

In "Networking Magic", authors Rick Frishman and Jill Lublin keep stressing these words: "network with the best." They're right. Why limit yourself? In many European countries people have a "just behave normally, that's already crazy enough" mentality. Get yourself over this attitude. Follow your passion. Make sure you have the best network possible to help you live your passion. However, many of us fear contacting the "best people."

The easiest way to reach the best people begins with realizing that the world is constantly changing, and also with realizing that there are lots of opportunities. As with most things in life, a step-by-step approach can be applied to finding the best people.

In this case this step-by-step process could look like this:

1. **Locate the best people in your network to help you reach your goals.** Since you already know them, contacting them is relatively safe. You don't have to go out of your comfort zone too much. This will build confidence and trust in the process of contacting the best people.

2. **Then ask yourself "is this person really the best person to help me?"** While being in the process of finding the best people, you might get more insights into who is really the best person for you.

   Maybe you realize that someone else from your current network can help you even better than your current number one.

3. **When you're comfortable dealing with the best people from your existing network, it is time to look outside your network.** Ask yourself: "Who is the best person in my area, field of expertise, industry?" It might be time for the next expert to become part of your network.

4. **Repeat steps 2 and 3** the rest of your life

Important note: don't waste too much time finding the "best of the best" from the beginning. Just take the first step. Look for the one who is best for you at this moment. It is likely that this will change in the future. Don't wait for it. Begin your networking journey with the "best people" you currently know. Many tennis players have outgrown their initial coaches. That's normal. Some coaches are better in teaching the basics, other in the details that make the difference between the number 13 and the number five position in the world ranking. But you will never get to number five without the basics.

***Networking success tip: don't only look for the people who can help you to reach your goals, but also with other things in your personal and professional life: who is the best plumber, who is the best travel agent, who is the best baker, who is the best information provider, who is the best insurance agent and even who is the best networker.***

***Jim Rohn: Don't join an easy crowd. You won't grow. Go where the expectations and the demands to perform are high.***

# Chapter 2

# Insights in networking

For many people networking has a negative connotation. Most likely the reason is that they encountered a "hard seller" at a networking event. In this chapter you will learn the difference between networking and hard selling. For most people reading this part is a relief because networking comes more naturally to them than hard selling. Even for the ones that are hard sellers at the time they read it.

You will also read my opinion in the discussion about what's most important in networking: quality or quantity.

First we start by looking at the "6 degrees of proximity," the phenomenon that causes us to say, "It's a small world" when we discover common contacts when meeting someone new. The 6 degrees of proximity principle shows the real power of networking. Tap into this power and your (business) life will be much easier!

## 6 degrees of proximity

### It's a small world

Remember the last time you were on vacation and you met some of your compatriots. Ten to one you discovered in your conversation that you had a common contact. This happens a lot on vacations, even more than in "normal" daily life. Why is this?

The first reason is that it IS a small world and the second is that you took the time to explore the different ways you are related to each other.

On vacations we are more relaxed. We are more open and more patient to listen. Moreover, since we don't know the people we just met yet, we are still open and ready to explore ALL different areas of life.

When we meet other people in daily life it is almost always in a specific environment: colleagues at the office, business contacts at networking events, family at birthday parties...In these environments we have a common interest that is already established, just by the nature of this context. That's the reason why we tend to limit our information exchange and search for more common ground to (the topics of) this specific environment. Once we talked to people, we have put them in one or more categories in our minds (and/or in our databases). This is very normal behavior. This is necessary for us to cope with all the information that we are bombarded with on a continuous basis. The disadvantage is that we only know snippets of people's lives and miss lots of opportunities or interesting conversations. We also tend to talk about the subjects we already know this person is interested in. But, everything changes, including us and all people from our network at an ever-increasing pace.

Because we are only capable of knowing "parts" of other people, we are still surprised when we find out that we have something in common with someone. "It's a small world" you hear from time to time (and this becomes a daily standard phrase when you become a real networker). When two people discover that it is a small world indeed, you feel the atmosphere change. Suddenly there is more room for a relaxed posture, fun and trust.

In reality we indeed live in a small world. We are connected to everyone – EVERYONE on this planet via six people. This phenomenon is called the "6 degrees of separation." In this network era where people are reconnecting, I'd like to change this name into "6 degrees of proximity." If you can contact anyone on this earth via a maximum of six steps, then you are close and related to each other, instead of separated, don't you agree?

The *"Small World Experiment,"* by Stanley Milgram in 1967 has given way to this belief of being connected to everyone else in the world via six steps. In short, the experiment went as follows: Stanley Milgram randomly selected people in the Midwest to send packages to a stranger located in Massachusetts. The senders knew the recipient's name, occupation, and general location. They were instructed to send the package to a person they knew on a first-name basis who they thought was most likely, out of all their friends, to know the target personally. That person would then do the same, and so on, until the package was personally delivered to its target recipient. Although the researchers expected the chain to include at least a hundred intermediaries, it only took on average six intermediaries to get each package delivered.

Although the results of his experiment were not scientifically founded (the test population was too small and participation was very low), other experiments showed that it is indeed a small world. One of them was the experiment of Duncan Watts. In 2001, Watts, a professor at Columbia University, continued his own earlier research into the phenomenon and recreated Milgram's experiment on the Internet. Watts used an email message as the "package" that needed to be delivered, and surprisingly, after reviewing the data collected by 48,000 senders and 19 targets (in 157 countries), Watts found that the average number of intermediaries was, indeed, six.

One example of how the "6 degrees of proximity" works in practice is the networking website LinkedIn (www.linkedin.com). On this website you can see how many people you have in your direct network and with how many people you are connected through them. We explore LinkedIn deeper in the chapter about online networking (see page 197).

Another example is the "Oracle" of the University of Virginia. The "Oracle" contains the names of actors, actresses and directors from all (or at least the most) movies from all over the world. You can then see via how many – or better, how few – steps two actors are linked. Try it yourself one time, it's fun: www.cs.virginia.edu/oracle/

Let me also share with you an example of the small world phenomenon I experienced myself. In 2004, I came in contact with Melissa Giovagnoli, the author of Networlding, through the website Ecademy (www.ecademy.com). At the time of writing, Melissa lived in Chicago, USA and I lived in Rumst, Belgium (Europe). We only had contact via the Ecademy website, email and phone. In March 2005, creativity consultant, Gregg Fraley, was a keynote speaker at a congress in Belgium. During the reception I spoke with him (I always make contact with speakers at events and I advise you to do this, too!) and though this was his first visit to Belgium and I never visited the United States before, we still had a contact in common: Melissa Giovagnoli. Gregg also lives in Chicago and knew Melissa in person. We both laughed about this "small world" example and had a nice conversation.

## The 6 degrees of proximity in numbers

Let's look at the "6 degrees of proximity" from another point of view. In many books about networking (like "Power Networking" by Donna Fisher and Sandy Vilas), you can read that everyone has an average of 250 contacts. Of course, this is an average; older salespeople will have many more contacts, babies have only a few.

If we do the math, this again shows that it really is a small world. Let's also assume that with everybody from your network, you have half of your contacts in common (which in reality isn't so, but let's have a conservative approach on this).

This means:

- First degree (your own network of direct contacts): 250 contacts
- Second degree (the direct contacts of your network that you don't know yourself): 250 x 125 contacts = 31,250 contacts
- Third degree: 31,250 x 125 contacts = 3,906,250 contacts

- Fourth degree: 3,906,250 x 125 contacts = 488,281,250 contacts
- Fifth degree: 488,281,250 x 125 contacts = 61,035,156,250 contacts
- Sixth degree: 61,035,156,250 x 125 contacts = 7,629,394,531,250 contacts

This is even more than there are people on the planet. So, in principle you could stop at degree five, but there are reasons why the math is only an average and we have to go a step further from time to time. Some of them are:

- Geography: people in countries on the other side of the globe are less likely to be closely connected to each other. The density of the population and the state of communication technology in a particular country also play an important role.

- Decreasing effectiveness of a higher degree: the further someone is away from you, the more "noise" sneaks in the message. When you were a kid you probably played the game where a story is whispered in your neighbor's ear (also called "Chinese whisper"). At the end of the chain the original story is usually completely modified. Even more important is that the chain of trust becomes "weaker." A friend of a friend will do something for you because you both have a strong connection with mutual friend, but the further you go, the "weaker" this bond is, and the lower the chance of a response.

- Connectors and loners: some people are heavily connected with links to thousands of people. Others tend to shy away from society. It's obvious that a connector can help you to reduce the amount of degrees drastically. A loner could be a very interesting person, but won't contribute much with regard to new contacts.

## The consequences of the 6 degrees of proximity

### *It's easy to find the best people to help you reach your goals*

If we are indeed connected to everyone else on the WHOLE PLANET via maximum six other persons, in how many or how few steps are we connected to the people we need to reach our goals?

Most of us still work and live in a relatively small geographic area, so probably the people that can help us best, are only maximum three to four steps away from us. If you approach them wisely, the contacts from your network should be able to bring you in contact with them (see also "How to approach the "best people" for your network?" on page 42).

## *Improve your "results" at networking events*

Another consequence of the 6 degrees of proximity principle is that it allows us to step away from the "taker" mentality and take on a "giver" attitude.

Let me explain this with an example. In April 2005, I was one of the speakers at a congress of IT hardware resellers in Belgium. There were approximately 80 people in my session. When I asked them who had the "authority to make sales decisions" 80% of the people raised their hands. When I asked who had "authority to make a buying decision," only 30% raised their hands. Then I told them "if you are here to do direct business with each other, I wish the 80% good luck to find out who those 30% are and who are not yet in a conversation with another seller. If you are a buyer, I wish you lots of patience and inspiration to escape from this mass of salesmen." (In case you're wondering about the 80% and 30%: 10% of the participants were small business owners who had the authority to both sell and buy).

Of course, this is a rather extreme point of view. I know that most salesmen (and because I have to sell my services and books, I'm a salesman, too) are not going to stalk the buyers, but I wanted to make my point with regard to the "6 degrees of proximity."

If you look at it from a "small world" point of view, then everybody in that room represented on average 31,250 direct contacts (first and second degree). If they would talk to each other to see if and how they could help each other buy or sell to their respective networks, not only would there be more business, but also the atmosphere in the room would change.

The high energy that comes from becoming aware of this mass of opportunities is very contagious, and you get the opportunity to build a relationship. We are always suspicious or even reluctant to strangers that want to sell their products or services, but we "lower our guard" to people who try to help us (or our network) to accomplish something without necessarily expecting anything in return.

Before you start emailing me with the question, "Does this mean I can't do any business at events anymore?" Let me reassure you: you don't have to hesitate when you meet someone you can do business with. My message is: instead of focusing on direct business, look for ways how your network can be of service to them and vice versa. If an opportunity to do business arises, people will be even more willing to do business with you as a result of your attitude.

***Networking success tip: If you are not trying to sell your stuff and you are not focused on yourself, but just look for ways to help your contact and your network to do business, people will pick up on this and feel more relaxed around you. Therefore, they will be more willing to connect with you.***

## *Build a large "sleeping customer file"*

In my sales function I have always tried to build relationships with people, not directly sell my products or services. As a result, I have a large "sleeping customer file" as Sharon Drew Morgen calls this phenomenon in her book, "Selling with Integrity."

In practice this means that when I have a conversation with prospects, I always listen to what they need at this moment or what kind of projects they are doing right now. I don't try to sell my services. Most of the time I don't even talk about what I offer unless they ask me.

What I focus on is matching my prospects with people from my network.

If I find a match the prospect is happy because I have a potential solution for his/her current problem and my network contact is happy, because he/she gets a hot referral. Then what's in it for me?

I can ask both of them to give me warm or hot referrals. This is a very powerful way to tap into the power of networking. Give it a try!

Personally, I don't ask for a referral every time. Making two people happy satisfies me enough.

Before you think I'm a modern Mother Theresa (but again, maybe I am) and that this is crazy, non-commercial behavior, think of the "Give and Receive" concept.

Let me give you an example.

I was in contact with Veerle Koks, one of the training consultants at Alcatel in Belgium. We already had a few telephone conversations and I had given her some names and contact data of other trainers that could be useful to her. They were also considering hiring me to train their co-workers to become better networkers, but it was not high on their priority list. One day there was this meeting of the VOV, the organization that represents the Human Development and Training managers in Flanders (Belgium). During a break I was sharing a table with some other people and we introduced ourselves to each other. One of them, Dany Vissers of the Vlaamse Gemeenschap (government of Flanders) asked me: "Are you thé Jan Vermeiren?" Although my ego was flattered, I didn't want to brag about myself, so I said: "Yes, my name is Jan Vermeiren, but I'm not sure you're talking to the one you had in mind, because there are other people with the same name." And he asked me: "The networking expert?" Then I had to admit that he wasn't mistaken. And, curious as I am, I asked him: "How do you know me?" He responded: "I just met Veerle Koks of Alcatel and she strongly recommended that I see you with regard to my search for a networking coach for some of our managers." The "Give and Receive" boomerang I had thrown to Alcatel came back to me, at a moment in time and from an angle I never could have foreseen.

Although this example has a strong sales focus, this can also be applied in other circumstances and environments. If you are a fan of a local restaurant, ask for business cards you can distribute to your friends. Both will be happy. Or if you have a terrific plumber, share this information with your neighbors and family. Spread the word and in the end the word about you will also be spread.

## Some warnings about the 6 degrees of proximity

The principle of the 6 degrees of proximity is a very powerful one. It will help you to leverage your networking efforts. At the same time it has certain characteristics that require some of your attention.

The most powerful degrees are the first and second. On these levels there are still some personal relationships. You can build further on these relationships on third level and sometimes fourth works, too, but the fifth and sixth are usually too far away. Of course, you can change this situation. If you get in touch with someone that is now in the third degree and you really get to know each other, this person becomes a direct contact. Then the person that was originally six degrees away is now rather easy to reach via your new first degree contact.

Though it may be rather obvious to you that fifth and sixth degree are hard to approach, I wanted to warn you about this fact for the following reasons:

- Don't expect to get help from someone in the sixth degree. Especially when you use websites like LinkedIn. Be aware that it is difficult to get immediate help from someone who is more than three degrees away. Don't be angry if you get no response. Don't let this stop you from trying though. Never forget you're trying to build a relationship with them: how can you help them?

- It is important to take time to build relationships. Again, tools like LinkedIn seem to bypass many barriers and gatekeepers. They may also give you the false impression that you don't have to obey normal courtesy and relationship building processes anymore.

## Networking versus hard selling

### Farming versus hunting

A metaphor that is commonly used in books and articles about networking is that of the farm. It is the analogy of farming in contrast to hunting. Where networking is like farming and hard selling is like hunting. Stephen Covey uses another analogy in "The Seven Habits of Highly Effective People." He talks about products and production capability.

Let's see how the concept of the farm and that of Covey apply to networking.

Back in prehistoric days, people went out to hunt animals in order to have some food. Every time they killed a chicken, they had immediate food (product), but they were also obliged to go hunting the next day because they also killed a "production capability" for eggs. This is short-term thinking.

Later on our ancestors built farms where they grew crops and kept animals, not (only) for their meat, but for other products like eggs, milk or for breeding more animals. These small investments brought security and a higher level of prosperity. The investments didn't always guarantee a return. Diseases, floods, earthquakes and other tricks of nature caused many troubles. But by diversifying and looking at long-term results, and by knowing the power of the seasons, farmers benefited.

# Insights in Networking

A farmer knows that he can't expect to harvest in autumn when he didn't sow in spring. He also knows that when he sows many of those little seeds, the odds for a bigger harvest are much higher. So, what does he do? In spring he sows, in summer he nurtures and in autumn he reaps. Does he stop there? No, he prepares for the next year. He doesn't consume all corn; he keeps some of the seeds so they can be sown the next year.

It is the same with networking. You never know when and how things are going to come to you, but they will. The more seeds you plant, the higher the profits of your networking efforts. The better you nurture your relationships, the more willing they will be to help you benefit. And, last but not least, if your contacts with your network are good, you can always ask them for more "networking seeds." Meaning that you can always ask them for introductions and referrals.

To conclude the analogy with farming, I'd like to share an inspirational story from *"How to Talk Well"* from James Bender:

*"There was a farmer who grew award-winning corn. Each year he entered his corn in the state fair where it won a blue ribbon.*

*One year a newspaper reporter interviewed him and learned something interesting about how he grew it.*

*The reporter discovered that the farmer shared his seed corn with his neighbors. "How can you afford to share your best seed corn with your neighbors when they are entering corn in competition with yours each year?" the reporter asked.*

*"Why sir," said the farmer, "didn't you know? The wind picks up pollen from the ripening corn and swirls it from field to field. If my neighbors grow inferior corn, cross-pollination will steadily degrade the quality of my corn. If I am to grow good corn, I must help my neighbors grow good corn."*

*He is very much aware of the connectedness of life. His corn cannot improve unless his neighbor's corn also improves.*

*So it is in other dimensions. Those who choose to be at peace must help their neighbors to be at peace. Those who choose to live well must help others to live well, for the value of a life is measured by the lives it touches. And those who choose to be happy must help others to find happiness, for the welfare of each is bound up with the welfare of all.*

*The lesson for each of us is this: if we are to grow good corn, we must help our neighbors grow good corn."*

And that's what networking is all about!

## The difference between hard selling and networking

Though you already know that networking is more like farming and hard selling like hunting, I want to go a little deeper into the differences between networking and hard selling. Why? Networking sometimes has a negative connotation for people. This is due to the fact that many salesmen abuse networking to push their products or services.

The main difference between selling and networking is that in a sales process the goal of the interaction between two people is the sale of a product or service. When networking, this sale could be the consequence of a contact that is built with respect and care. It is clear that the sale is not the goal of networking, but a nice and, in many cases, a logical consequence.

The comparison in the table (below) goes into the details of the difference between selling and networking. The table shows several elements of "negative networking" by hard sellers and "real networking."

## Insights in Networking

| | Hard sellers who network... | Real networkers... |
|---|---|---|
| 1 | Are focused on the **short term** | Are focused on the **long term** |
| 2 | Try to **detect a need** that can be satisfied by their product or service | **Share any information** that can be interesting for the other party |
| 3 | **Only give when they have an immediate profit** | **Give without expecting something back** (and in the long run this usually pays off better, too) |
| 4 | **Listen in order to get the deal** | **Listen to help** |
| 5 | Ask questions in order to be able to **position** their product or service better | Ask questions to be able to be of better **assistance** |
| 6 | Find people interesting only if they are a **potential customer** | Find **everybody** interesting as a contact. You can never be certain of whom they know and what they know |
| 7 | Want to collect and distribute **as many business cards as possible** | Ask for and give business cards to people with whom **they really established contact** |
| 8 | Talk often only about their product or service **without listening to others** | See to it that **others always talk** more than they do, **listen carefully** to them and encourage them to tell more |
| 9 | Try to bring the **attention to their product or service** | **Recommend products or services of people in their network** (and only if they are relevant for the people they talk to) |
| 10 | **The goal is the sale.** People are a means, a resource (sometimes even a necessary evil) to reach that goal | **The goal is to establish and maintain contacts.** One of the **possible consequences is a sale** |

To make it even clearer, I have an example for you.

**Situation:** a salesman of fire extinguishers meets the manager of a local affiliate of a bank at a reception of the Chamber of Commerce.

***Hard Selling***

*The salesman does his sales magic to convince the manager to buy fire extinguishers for his office. He is a good salesman and he manages to sell five fire extinguishers.*

*The evening of the salesman is a success.*

***Networking***

*The salesman is interested in the manager as a person. Among other things, he learns that the manager is a passionate sailor and that he is looking for a new boat. The salesman remembers that a friend of his has a boat for sale. He not only passes this on to the manager, but also provides them with each other's contact details the following day. A week later the boat has a new owner.*

*Four months later, the salesman receives a phone call from the manager. The manager asks him to deliver new fire extinguishers for the office of the bank and for the facilities of the sailing club where the manager recently became chairman. Moreover, the manager proposes to write a letter to all the members of the sailing club with a recommendation for the fire extinguishers of the salesman.*

*The year of the salesman is a success.*

What about you? Are you more of a hard seller than a networker? You don't have to be a salesperson to be a seller. Everybody has to sell continuously. You have to "sell" the next project to your management team, you have to "sell" your time off to your colleagues, you have to "sell" to your partner to go to the movies instead of spending an evening at home, you have to "sell" to your children that they keep their room clean, you have to "sell" to your partner and/or colleagues that you want to go to the next networking event,... Everybody is a seller in one way or the other.

Let me repeat my question. What about you? Are you more of a hard seller or more of a networker?

## Quantity versus quality

What is the most important thing when networking? Quantity or quality? It's a topic that keeps people occupied. In my training courses there are always questions about this topic. In forums about networking on the Internet, this is always the start for a lively discussion.

### The importance of quality

Let me start by asking you a question: what is quality? How do you define it?

Many people perceive people in a high position in a large and well-known company as "high quality." Let's call such a person Ms. Big Shot. They do everything they can to come into contact with her when they see her at an event, but when they get a few minutes of this person's attention, they don't know what to say and focus on exchanging business cards.

Afterwards, they send emails and start calling Ms. Big Shot only to be blocked by her secretary. Then they are disappointed in Ms. Big Shot, in the event they attended and in networking in general.

Do you recognize this situation? Either from your own experience or from someone you know? Then it might be a good idea to look differently at "quality."

For me "quality" can only be measured when compared to your goals. A person is of "high quality" if she (or her network) can help you to reach your goals better and faster. Ms. Big Shot could be high quality, but she is also very busy, so it might be a good idea to look for other people of equal quality that are easier to approach and who have more time for you.

Quality is definitely important in networking, but so is quantity. Why?

## The importance of quantity

There are four major reasons why quantity is also important.

### *More opportunities*

A higher quantity of contacts gives you more opportunities to find "high quality" people. But again this means that you have to know your goals. I'm not a promoter of collecting as many contacts as you possibly can. At events and on the Internet you will see many people expanding their (virtual) address books. For some of them it's kind of a sport to be able to brag: "look at how many people I know." But when one of these contacts wants to deepen the relationship, they don't answer emails or phone calls. Don't get me wrong. There is nothing wrong with huge address books – as long as you are available to your network. If you're just collecting people like collecting stamps, it might be good to tell them that. This way there are no wrong expectations. Wrong expectations can harm your reputation, and that's the last thing you want in networking.

Having more opportunities also means that you have to rely less on luck or coincidence for things to happen in your life. Lots of contacts combined with knowing your goals will have

you experience more synchronicity in your life, too!

### *Your goals change over time*

As your goals change over time, the "quality" of people changes, too. Somebody who was of "low quality" a year ago could be number one today. Sometimes the opposite is true, so this is another reason why everybody is important.

For example: a former product manager of a large telecom company told me that he was never interested in meeting accountants and lawyers at events of the

Chamber of Commerce. Moreover, he ran away from them. Once he started his own company, he regretted the fact that he didn't have any connections in those two fields.

### *Value for your network*

Somebody might be of "low quality" for you, but of "high quality" for someone from your network. A good networking action is connecting people. By connecting them, you strengthen your relationship with both of them. This creates goodwill. They will both be more motivated to help you to find the "high quality" people you are looking for.

In fact, connecting people is one of the best networking actions you can do. It is free and you help two people at once. You will be remembered as a great help and, as a consequence, the chances increase that they will remember you when there is an opportunity in your field.

### *Diversity creates a larger safety net when circumstances change*

We all have the tendency to stick around people who have the same interests, the same background, the same education and other similar things. Wayne Baker calls this the "similarity principle." In his book, "Networking Smart," you will find many examples of this principle. Sometimes this tendency to stick around with the same people is good; sometimes it is a disadvantage. For example, when you are looking for a new job, it is better to have a large and diversified network. Your small core group will limit you to the same sources of information or job opportunities.

## Find your balance between quality and quantity

You now know that quantity and quality are both important. What should you do next? It's a cliché, but my advice is:

**Find your own balance between quality and quantity.**

Keep (most of) the business cards or electronic contact data of the people you meet. For me there are only a few exceptions to this rule. When people are rude, insincere or are just using me or other people, I'm not inclined to keep their data. I might, but only to remind myself never to do business with them, or never to introduce or refer them to other people.

***Networking success tip: never throw away a sincere person's business card.***

Remember that a person that is not "interesting" for you today might become very helpful towards your next goal. Considering the small world principle, you never know whom this person knows or how he could help somebody from your network.

***Networking success tip: with modern technology it is rather easy to store all contact data. However, keep the paper business cards as backup. In case you have a rather visual memory, it also helps you to better remember the people you have met.***

# Chapter 3

# Networking attitude in practice

In the previous chapters you laid your networking foundation and gained more insights in the dynamics of networking. In this chapter you will learn more about the fundamentals of the networking attitude. They consist of the Golden Triangle of networking, building trust and listening to people. You will not only gain more insights, but also get some very practical tips that you can use right away. Whether it is when networking at a reception, on the Web or with your current network, you can apply them everywhere!

## The Golden Triangle of networking

When I talk about the Golden Triangle of networking in presentations, people look at me like I'm talking about the Bermuda triangle. Perhaps the analogy isn't that far-fetched, but in the opposite way. Meaning: instead of mysterious disappearances, the Golden Triangle of networking generates unexpected opportunities. You can also call this synchronicity. These opportunities have a kind of magical entry in our lives, but there is nothing magical about it. It's a logical consequence of the implicit nature of real networking: if you give without expecting something back, you receive a lot more than you could imagine. Next to giving, the Golden Triangle consists of asking and thanking.

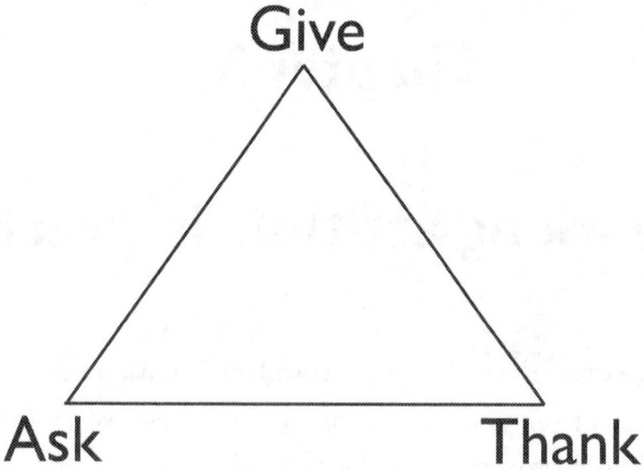


The hard part for many people in the whole networking concept is "giving without expecting anything in return." Let's use this topic as a start to unravel the secrets of the Golden Triangle of networking."

***Elizabeth Asquith Bibesco:***
***Give without remembering; receive without forgetting.***

## Giving

When I talk about giving, I mean something other than products or services. Products and services are what you want to sell in exchange for money. That's not unconditional. There is nothing wrong with that. On the contrary, it is what you need to make a living. "Giving" is about something you give away for free. It implies expecting nothing in return.

In my training courses, people tell me: "That is a nice idea, Mother Theresa, but this can't be working in practice, especially not for me. I don't have anything to offer to other people."

If you recognize this, this chapter is definitely for you. You get lots of tips and advice on how to offer something without expecting anything in return. Giving is very important. People like givers and shy away from takers.

Many people have a bad feeling with giving things away. This bad feeling comes from the discrepancy between what you invest (money, time or other resources) and what you get back.

**Satisfaction/Dissatisfaction = Benefit – Investment**

You get satisfaction when the benefit is greater than the investment – dissatisfaction when you feel you have invested more than it benefited you. The problem is: you can't always control what you get back. A solution is to work on the other end of the equation: minimize your investments. However, this doesn't mean that you give less "value" to the receiver. I call this approach the "low cost, high perceived value" method. Low cost for you, high perceived value for the receiver. This approach is about knowing what your added value is and knowing how to offer this in a cost and time efficient way.

Let's take a look at what you could give to other people with minimal investments. This will help you to offer something without expecting anything in return. The first two tips apply to everybody; the value of the rest of the suggestions depends on your professional situation.

## *Your network*

Your network is perhaps the asset with the highest perceived value and lowest cost you can offer to other contacts. It's free and it's something everybody can offer, in a professional and in a private context.

When I meet people, I always ask them what they are looking for at this moment in their personal and professional lives. Then I check my network to see if there is anyone who can help them directly or knows someone who can help them.

Linking two people in your network not only doesn't cost you any money and only a small amount of time, but it also strengthens your relationship with both parties. Do it as much as you can, you will be astonished by the results!

## *Things that anybody can offer at no cost*

• Specific knowledge about non-business stuff: the best restaurants in your hometown, specific vacation destinations (maybe you are a huge fan of Mexico), books, thrillers or food/drinks. Do you have a large collection of novels or a large science fiction movie collection? Is your lasagna the best in the world and are you willing to share the recipe? These are all things that you can offer to people. It shows that you are not only occupied with working, but that you are a human being with appealing personal interests.

- Send information to others that may be of value to them: articles from magazines or eZines (electronic magazines), website addresses, blogs.
- Advise: but don't patronize. Don't push other people to follow your opinion.
- Help overcome the fear of making new contacts: by inviting someone to an event and introducing him/her to other people.
- Recommend products and services that you like: especially (but, not exclusively) from partners, friends, suppliers, customers and network contacts.
- Share information: that you discovered by trial and error.
- Give feedback: about the ideas of others.
- Encourage people.
- Brainstorm: and contribute to ideas and concepts.
- Lend your ear: just by expressing your interest towards other people will improve your relationship with them.
- Learn what others do: so you can promote them and refer other people to them.
- Suggest a new idea or insight.

## *Samples and upgrades*

One of the best marketing tactics is to give away free samples of a physical or digital product. It helps to lower the barriers to building a relationship. Sometimes it is a "one-to-many" relationship between a company and its customers. Cosmetic companies use this tactic to build relationships. It is the beginning of building trust.

An example of a company that is doing more than giving away free samples is Vistaprint. On www.vistaprint.com you can order business cards for free!

These samples do cost money though. Only use them if you can afford them and don't have a bad feeling when giving them away for free.

Another variant of samples are "upgrades." This is something that airlines often do. They give you an upgrade for free or a low cost.

Peter Dalmeijer and Anita Van Ostaden told an example of another upgrade to me. They run the training and coaching company, Vidarte (www.vidarte.nl). They gave a two-day training seminar in the hotel De Zeeuwse Stromen in Renesse (The Netherlands). When they arrived, the manager offered them another room – the VIP room. For them it was a nice start of their stay at the hotel. Later that evening they were also offered a free newspaper and a free bag of candies. They really felt special and were very happy with this treatment. As a result, they are now recommending this hotel to other people and the example even found its way into this book. What did it cost the hotel? Almost nothing: another room (that wasn't occupied anyway), a newspaper, a bag of candies and some extra attention. This small upgrade has an enormous emotional leverage.

How can you "upgrade" your products or services? Even if you are not in sales or production, what emotional leverage with low financial cost can you create for your (internal) customers and colleagues?

## *Articles*

Many authors and trainers, including myself, give away samples of our material. We write articles about our expertise. If you write too, be smart and reuse as much as you can. If you wrote a book, you have enough material for many articles that can be posted at several websites or published in magazines. You can send the same article to many different websites. You can also make small (white) papers for your own website. This way you can regularly update your website. Recycling your own stuff lowers the "investment" (in time and money!) you have to make to give something of value to people. So, give this tip serious thought.

Don't be shy to send your articles to the press, especially to the Internet journalists. Press in general has a never ending need for new and interesting content. By sending them articles, you are giving them this content and helping them out. If you are not used to doing this, you could start with the journalists that have to deliver content for websites. Most of the time they have to operate in smaller teams and, as a consequence, need more contributions from other people, so it will be easier to get published. Another advantage of websites is that your article ends up in an online archive where people can find it, even if it was published more than a year ago. In my case, I even have some permanent files on networking on two of the largest websites in Belgium: www.tijdnet.be (a news site with strong economic emphasis) and www.vacature.be (a job site).

An article is great. When it gets published you at least get free publicity in return, and perhaps you will also start building a good relationship with journalists. Journalists are connectors. They have to be connectors in order to do their job. They need a large network to get their information. Connect with them!

Writing articles and papers doesn't have to be for a magazine or a website. Publishing articles on the intranet of your company will also give you visibility inside your company and helps to get other people interested in your expertise.

## *Free newsletter*

Many companies use a free electronic or paper newsletter to maintain the relationship with interested parties. This is a great idea if used in the right way. Lots of companies distribute a free "newsletter," but in fact, it is just publicity. It says: "look at me, look how good I am, bring your money to me..."

A good newsletter is less about you and more about your target group. It is important to write about things they are interested in. If you only want to sell your stuff, don't call your publication a "newsletter." The only exceptions are newsletters where offers are clearly indicated and separated from the content, from the real value for the average reader.

A newsletter should preferably contain three aspects:

1. Information
2. Education
3. Advice

Before you start writing your newsletter, you should know about the topics that interest your target group, your readers. Put yourself in their shoes. Empathize. Empathy is one of the traits we will need even more to be successful in the future. Then start writing. First you should **inform** your target audience about the things that are happening in their field of interest. Secondly, you **educate** them: "if event A occurs, then consequence B will be the result." Thirdly, you **advise** them: "if you know this, could it be that X is a good solution for you..." You don't have to write much about your own company and organization (in fact, doing that too much might turn against you). Your logo and name on the newsletter is enough to start building a relationship. That's the added value of a newsletter.

Again, you could reuse the content of articles you wrote for websites or parts of your book or papers.

Maybe you are reading this and thinking, "Writing newsletters is not for me, I don't have a company and I don't work in the marketing department of my organization." Then there is something else for you: blogging (see the part about "Blogs: what are they and what do they have to do with networking?" on page 184).

## *Checklists*

Another example on giving is that of a bridal shop near Antwerp (Belgium) where every visitor received a "Don't forget this on your wedding day" checklist.

The checklist reminded them about topics like flowers, rings, catering, photographer, church, party location,... The visitors were very happy to receive this checklist. Imagine forgetting something on the most important day of your life!

### *What's so good about checklists?*

For the bridal shop the costs were minimal: it took only 20 minutes to write the items down, and some layout work. Printing could be done on their own small printer. The actual costs are low, but the customers perceived this as high value. It is a perfect win-win situation. Because of the low cost the bridal shop happily hands out the checklists without expecting anything back.

If you are in charge of marketing, you could learn something else from this bridal shop. They didn't only list the things you shouldn't forget for your wedding, but also added the names of shops and companies who could provide these items. The visitors didn't have to look for suppliers themselves. The bridal shop involved its network and included them in the success.

### *The concept behind a checklist*

What exactly did the people from the bridal shop do?

They put some of the knowledge inside their heads (the so-called "tacit knowledge") on paper and made it "explicit."

How does this apply to your situation? To what extent can you make your expert knowledge available to others in order to help them and have something of value you can give away without expecting something back? You don't have to write everything you know down, but make sure you have a "low cost (for you), high perceived value" item for the people of your network.

Again, this example also applies if you don't have much interaction with the world outside your company. Write a checklist for your colleagues. Write a checklist for new people in your local community or (sports) club.

### *eCourse*

Let's look at another example: my own networking eCourse. What's an eCourse? An eCourse is a series of emails about a specific topic. In my case, a series of 15 emails with tips about networking.

My eCourse cost me an investment of 2.5 days. It took one day to figure out the technology behind it (this technology is called "autoresponder" and is heavily recommended if you are responsible for the marketing in your organization). Then it took 1.5 days to write the content and put it in the system. Now it's up and running and I don't have to do anything anymore.

For me it was a relatively low cost (2.5 days of work) and for the subscribers it has a high value.

I can give the eCourse away for free, without having bad feelings about it or without expecting anything back. Why? – I don't have to spend any more time or money on it.

You can subscribe to the eCourse on my website www.networking-coach.com

### *Your expertise*

All the previous examples are about offering your expertise in some way of written form (a checklist, an article, an eCourse, a newsletter…). You can also offer your expertise in other ways.

In one of my training courses for Alcatel, one of the participants offered his expertise to his network in two domains:

1. His experiences with working abroad in lots of different countries made him a valuable contact for other employees with regard to the administrative part as well as for local customs and tips and advice.
2. As a long-standing member of a "beer tasting" club, he could offer advice on how to organize a "beer tasting" night and which beers to choose. I must honestly admit that I've long forgotten what his technical experience at Alcatel is, but I'm sure I'm not the only one who remembers his international experience and expertise in beer!

### *How about you?*

The reason why we refrain from giving is that we sometimes have a bad feeling about it. You only have this bad feeling if you feel that you are out of balance. That it's too much "trouble" for you to help the other person without ever getting anything back.

If you think about the examples I gave you, you'll surely find something that applies to you.

What can YOU do? What can YOU offer without expecting anything back?

Remember: networking is a game that is always played by two parties and in the long run, you reap what you sow. So start sowing (offering) so you can reap more and faster!

***Winston Churchill: "We make a life by what we give."***

## Asking

### *How do you feel when making a request?*

Many people hesitate to involve their network in a request. What about you? Do you find it difficult to ask a question?

Are you also thinking: "Will they have time for me? Who am I to ask a question? Will they know the answer? Will anybody be able to help me? Will anybody be willing to help me? Will they know anybody who can help me? What will they ask in return?" Or do you think: "I have to be able to do this on my own," "I don't need anyone's help," "I don't want to bother people," "I don't know them well enough to call them." "People will think I'm weak/needy/stupid if I approach them about this." "I have no right to expect others to help me out" or "I don't want them to realize I need help with this."

Then your inner thoughts may prevent you from enjoying the powers of networking.

Let me ask you a question. If somebody asks you for advice or asks you to do him a favor and you really can help him out, what kind of feeling do you get? A negative or neutral one or a positive one? I think we can agree on a positive feeling: warm, happy, satisfied,... We all want to contribute. It is human nature to help each other.

If we reverse this thought, we could say that by NOT making a request to our network, we deprive them of the chance to help us and to get a positive feeling.

So what are you waiting for? Start asking questions and make other people feel good!

In order to give you a head start, I will give you some more tips: what is a good question and how do you phrase it?

## *What does a good question look like?*

A good question is like a good goal: it has to be as specific as possible – the more specific the better. Compare it with a search engine like Google. When you enter the word "networking" you get 178,000,000 hits (on March 6, 2007). Let's assume you are looking for a networking coach. You begin to scroll down and look at the results. After half an hour you are tired and frustrated because you didn't find what you were looking for. If you start a new search with the exact phrase "networking coach" you only get 11,400 results. The odds that you find what you are looking for have increased substantially! Do the same with your requests: make them more specific.

Another example: a friend of mine lost his job and asked me: "You have lots of contacts, can you help me to get a new job?" I probably could have helped him, but where on earth should I have started? This question was so vague that I was not able to help him.

So, what did I do? I asked questions: what experience do you have, which languages do you speak, what are your goals, what is your added value to an organization, what are your expectations and in which region do you want to work? We finally got to the point where I could help him. It became clear that he had six years experience in IT, more specifically programming in Visual Basic, C++ and.Net, was trilingual (Dutch, French, English) and was looking for a company in the vicinity of Antwerp. This narrowed the search in my brain and in my database, and then I was able to introduce him to two potential employers.

***Networking success tip: help others to help you. Be specific!***

If you want a good answer: ask a good question. Prepare yourself. Think about what you want and how other people can contribute to reaching your goal. That way you give the signal that you made some effort yourself to get the best possible answer. People appreciate this, and they don't always appreciate you using their time to "prepare yourself."

An exception to this warning is when you explicitly ask someone to help you to get your questions clear. Sometimes I "use" two friends of mine: Wim Van Acker (www.wimvanacker.com) or Cees De Bruin (www.notthecarrot.com) to ask me questions. They are excellent at doing this. I always get new insights, just by answering their questions. I recommend them both!

> ***Networking success tip: help others to get their questions as specific as possible.***

## *Attention points when making requests*

### *The right moment*

Before asking a question it is always good to check if the person has time for you. Contrary to what most people believe, it is OK to directly say what you are calling for. I used to say "Am I disturbing you?" which already indicated that I didn't find my question important enough or valued the other person's time more important than mine, but with my weak opener I already opened the gate to "failure."

In her book, "Selling with Integrity" Sharon Drew Morgen gives examples of how to avoid this. She advices sales people to use these words: "This is Sharon Drew Morgen speaking. This is a sales call. Is this a good time for you to talk?" When I first read this, I couldn't believe this would work, but when I tried it myself, I couldn't believe the results. People were surprised by my honesty and no one ever told me that he was not interested. If it was not a good time for them, they gave me another time to call them back.

"But I'm not a salesperson," you probably think. Still this also applies to you. I use variants of this sentence in all my communication, personal or professional. "Hi mom, I'm just calling to say hello. Is it a good time for you to talk?" or "Hi, business partner X, I'm calling about the contract. Is this a good time for you to discuss this?" By using this phrase you show that you are confident about what you want and respect other people's time. Just try it!

### *Acknowledge the other person*

There is one other important thing most people forget to do when asking questions: telling the person they contact why they chose them. Ask yourself this question: when you are looking for a plumber, why do you ask Uncle Jim and not your neighbor or any other contact from your network?

Because you know Uncle Jim has better relationships in this field, has more experience, knows which plumber is specialized in what kind of job, or is more trustworthy in these matters than anyone else you know. But when you call him, do you tell him how much you respect him and his expert level?

People like small compliments. Do Uncle Jim a favor by making one (but always be sincere, otherwise this might turn against you!) By telling him how much you "admire" him, you create a very constructive atmosphere, where his willingness to listen to your question will increase. You will definitely get a solution, in one way or the other.

## *Some more tips about asking*

Here is a list of tips that will make it easier for you to ask a question:

- **Be clear about what you want and need:** Don't hint, don't suggest and don't hope. ASK!
- **Be short:** Too much information can cause your real question to get covered up in the mass of words. A good idea is to state your question shortly and clearly, and then give some background information. Don't hide your question in a long and – sometimes for the other person, boring story.
- **Be strong:** Don't ask because you're needy or desperate. Don't ask with a complaining voice. Asking a question means that you want to learn and want to grow. That is a very positive point, not something you have to lose sleep over.
- **Ask with the expectation that you'll receive what you want:** Honor the other person by taking a positive point of view about his ability to help you.
- **Give people the opportunity to respond:** Ask something and then be silent for a moment allowing the other person to reflect on this and give a response,

especially if you have the tendency to weaken your question. Many people start strong, but before the other person has the opportunity to answer, they add…"if it's not that much trouble for you, otherwise I'll do it myself." Subconsciously this sends out two messages:

1. you don't really value the other person's ability to help you.
2. you are not a person who values the Golden Triangle of networking and, therefore, not the best person to keep networking with in the future.

- **Ask in such a way that people see the opportunities for you and the importance of their reaction:** Share your dream or goal with them. Say this in a way they feel your passion. Passion is very contagious. Only a few people really turn down passionate people. Almost everyone will try to help you out, one way or the other.

## *The best question in networking*

Many people not only have a problem asking questions, but once they exceed that threshold, they also have a problem with asking a direct question. "Direct" in the meaning of: making a request to the person who has the authority to make a decision. It has nothing to do with an open or closed question so don't get confused.

I have some good news for the people fearing to address a person in a direct way: the best question in networking is an "indirect" one!

Let's take a look where this "best question" comes from.

**Step 1: from a "direct" to an "indirect" question**

For example, instead of asking: "Will you hire me as a marketing assistant?" you can ask: "Do you know anyone who is looking for a new marketing assistant?"

If this person is looking for a new marketing assistant, he will tell you. If not, you have **triggered his mind into thinking of other people who might be able to help you.**

Another benefit of this question is that you give the other person the possibility to say "no" to your request (hiring you) without jeopardizing the relationship between the two of you. You give him the opportunity to help you in another way: introducing you to someone else or giving you other tips to reach your goal.

**Step 2: from an "indirect" question to the best question in networking**

The previous "indirect" question is already a huge step in the right direction, but the "best question" would be: "Who do you think I should contact when looking for a new job as a marketing assistant?"

This way you not only ask an indirect question, but you also have the possibility to **receive a whole list of good contacts that may refer you to people in their network.** You also broaden your possibilities. Maybe your contact doesn't know any marketing directors, but one of his best friends could be the editor of a marketing magazine.

In other words, the best and safest question to ask your network is:

> ***"Who do you think I should contact in respect to . . ." + your specific question***

You will be surprised with the results of this approach. Do me and especially yourself a favor and try it!

To encourage you to really do this, I want to share this story with you:

In July 2005, I had lunch with change management consultant, Han Juch of AlterMate. He told me that my advice about approaching people had worked. In the past he had difficulty getting appointments with potential customers, but now he had contacted some companies to ask them if they knew someone who would benefit from his specific experience in setting up and maintaining "the second organization," a specific concept of his about change management. The companies he contacted "lowered their guard" and were willing to listen to his story and to help him look for customers. After his meetings, two of the three companies he visited were interested themselves in his concept and his experiences at other companies. They wanted to introduce him to people from their network as well!

Networking success tip: if you want to move ahead in your professional and personal life and give your network the opportunity to assist you, it is important to ask regularly and in a respectful way!

## *Getting requests: the power of saying "no"*

In my training courses, one of the most frequently asked questions is: "How do I find the time to build and maintain my network?"

First of all, it is important to understand that your network should somehow be beneficial to you and certainly not be a waste of your time. A benefit doesn't necessarily have to be business. In life it is important to have a balance. So, a benefit of your network could also be having a drink, doing sports or spending time with family.

However, when you are in the stage of building your network, more likely than not, you will have to invest some time without always having a short-term benefit. In the long run, you will harvest the fruits of this investment.

For example: when you start going to meetings of your local Chamber of Commerce (or another organization) you will have to spend some time to get to know the other members and the organizers. They'll need to get to know you. If you have presented yourself clearly and don't have a "hard seller" attitude, they will after a few meetings start introducing and referring you to other attendees spontaneously. They will put you in touch with the people you are looking for, even without doing business with you themselves. Of course, this will happen a lot faster if you do this yourself for others.

Secondly, it is very important to think about how you spend your time. Time is the most democratic thing in the world. Everybody has 24 hours in a day. You can't buy any more time for yourself. But you can leverage the time you spend with people, your own time and the time of the people from your network.

Consider for a moment all aspects of your life – personal and professional. Are you enjoying every moment? No? What are those moments you enjoy less? These are the moments that are the first to be considered for outsourcing or exchanging with others. Don't hesitate to do this, even when you think, "I hate to do this, and I don't wish anybody else to do a boring job like this." Why? We are all different people. The things you like and dislike are different than mine or than somebody else's. Just ask if somebody wants to do this in your place. If you're smart, you already thought of what you could do or give in return. This will make the "exchange" a lot easier and more enjoyable.

Now, take a look at all the networking events you visited until now. Did you enjoy them? Were they interesting? Were they worth your time? Maybe there are other events that are more valuable to you. How do you choose between all the options you have?

The main reason why people perceive networking events as not interesting is that they didn't check the events off against their goals and values! Therefore, it is primordial to know your goals and values and preferably have them written on paper.

> ***Networking success tip: Before you can make a good judgment about what to do, where to spend your time and what to outsource/exchange, you need certain criteria. These are your goals and values.***

Thirdly, I see lots of people doing everything for members of their network (colleagues, bosses, family, friends...) and exhausting themselves. They keep going the extra mile without taking a break for themselves. They even spend time looking things up, making or buying stuff and doing all kinds of activities they hardly know anything about.

Their biggest "handicap" is that they find it very hard to say "no." That's not hard to understand. We all want to nourish our relationships. We don't want to disappoint them or we don't want to lose them as friends or business partners. However, running around like a chicken without a head, doesn't give a nice feeling either. Very commonly those people don't feel appreciated and start complaining because they don't see how they can turn this situation around. Suddenly they find themselves in a downward spiral. What do you do about this? The secret is actually very simple: **"say no, but give an alternative."**

For example, when people contact me and ask me something about networking or marketing, I will give them a detailed answer. Since these are my two areas of expertise it doesn't cost me much time or effort to formulate an answer myself or to send an article or to point out a website.

So, **when it's in my field of expertise, I always say "yes."**

When people contact me for something else other than networking or marketing, I say **"I'm sorry, my expertise is in networking and in marketing, so I can't help you. But give me a minute and I'll give you the name of someone who might help you or knows someone who can help you."** Then I look for the expert in the requested field or who is most likely to know the expert in my Outlook contacts. Then I introduce those two people to each other, preferably by email.

With this one sentence I accomplish following things.

- **I say "no," but I still help my contact.** The relationship is reinforced and I feel good about helping and about spending my time wisely.
- **I emphasize what my expertise is.** This is a subtle reminder for my contacts, especially if you have a tendency to change jobs, projects or interests.

This is a good way to let other people know what they can contact you for (and in what area they can refer people to you).

- **My relationship with the third party improves.** Because of the potential business deal, or at least because of the recognition of his/her expertise.

In short: when I get a question that is not in my field of expertise, I say, "I'm sorry I can't help you myself," but I always look for an alternative.

How about you? When was the last time you said "no," felt good about it, and didn't blow your relationship? Try the technique I described. You will feel better because you set your boundaries. Contrary to what you might expect, people will respect you more when you do this. People respect people who know what they want and who are aware of their strengths and weaknesses. You will have to spend less time on things you don't like and more time on the things you want.

## Thanking

Most of us do thank people when we receive something or when someone delivered a solution to a problem, but do we always thank people if we do NOT get something? Do you always thank someone when they took the time to look for a solution, but didn't find one? Or when they just took the time to listen to you?

Maybe you also recognize the following story. One of the things I still have difficulty with myself is remembering to thank people who introduced or referred me a long time ago. Let me explain this a little more. I got the name of a contact person at company X in January from a networking contact. They were interested in training their people in networking. Time went by and there were a few contacts, but still no course, until December. Then I got the phone call where my contact asked me to do a networking training course for his company.

I'm a bit ashamed to admit that I forgot to thank the initiator of this contact. It's so important to do this, even when months go by and lots of other projects and events intervene. Just by doing this small effort, you strengthen the relationship and keep your contact involved in your successes. This way he is encouraged to help you even more.

Another reason to thank people is:

**If you never thank someone, the other party's pleasure and satisfaction will slowly fade away.**

What do you have to take into account when thanking people? I have three tips for you.

## *Be specific*

Also, in thanking it is important to be as specific as possible to have the highest impact and to really nurture the relationship. Read the two following sentences and feel what appeals most to you:

- Tom, thanks for the good work!
- Tom, thanks for reviewing the offer we made for customer X. Your alternative solution to the payment and delivery terms not only got us the contract, but also saved us 5% on stock management. I really appreciate that you took the time to do this and spent four extra hours at the office on top of your own work. This really shows your commitment and your creativity.

Why does the second one feel better? It is more specific, more "tailor-made" and more credible. The person who said this, clearly thought about this compliment. It is not a compliment that can be given to anyone. Now Tom feels more appreciated. It is a small time investment, but a large deposit in the relationship account.

The second one also feels better because the behavior of Tom and his qualities were acknowledged.

When complimenting, give positive feedback concerning values, strengths and inherent talents. Do the same for the way people use these strengths and talents to realize things. I'd like to call this "giving feed forward." All too often, we get comments about what's not good, about what could be better. The word "feed forward" has a very positive connotation with the emphasis on strengths and future accomplishments.

### *Accept compliments*

On the other hand, if you are the one who gets a "thank you" note or compliment, be ready, willing and happy to receive it. Nothing would be more frustrating for Tom's manager than after sincerely thanking Tom getting the response, "Oh, it was nothing."

People who use these kinds of words in their response to a compliment are usually also the ones who complain about not being appreciated enough. They don't realize the relationship between accepting compliments and receiving them. If Tom tells his manager three times, "Oh, it was not that much trouble," then his manager doesn't feel appreciated for complimenting Tom. Then he will stop thanking him, or at least complimenting becomes a superficial habit with meaningless words. Even worse, if it is really no big trouble for Tom, why is the manager paying Tom to work for him? Wouldn't he better off looking for another, cheaper person who seems to be more motivated?

What about you? How do you respond when someone thanks you? Which answer from the list below do you normally use? How do you say it? Do you say it in a standard, meaningless way? Or with a smile, while looking in the other person's eyes?

Responses to compliments:

- "Oh, it's nothing"
- "That's part of the job"
- "Anyone could have done this"

- "You're welcome"
- "Thank you"
- "It was a pleasure to do this for you"

If you normally use one of the first three answers, try to change them into one of the other three, and do this consciously. Don't give up after one try, do this for a week and you will experience the difference!

## *Ways to thank people*

What do you prefer? – Giving or receiving a present. Most people even like giving a present more than receiving one.

What about receiving? In most cases, it doesn't matter what the present is or how much it costs. The simple fact of receiving a present is usually enough. Just the basic thought that somebody remembered us and made an effort to arrange a present makes it worthwhile. With this in mind there are many options for you to strengthen your relationships by giving "presents."

### *Say "Thank you"*

In business and in personal life a simple "thank you" could be enough, but by making a small extra effort you will stand out from the crowd.

### *Write a "thank you" note*

One of the things that faded away with the steep climb of the usage of email is writing letters and thank you notes. Reintroduce it in your own life. Writing by hand takes a little more time and effort than writing an email or making a phone call, but is also appreciated more. It is definitely worth the effort!

In his article, "The Power of a Note" (published in Reader's Digest magazine) Fred Bauer recommends four S's when writing a "thank you note:"

- **Sincere:** let it come from your heart
- **Short:** between one and three sentences (it is a note, not a letter)
- **Specific:** instead of "nice presentation:" "I was impressed by the way you linked the theory of Mintzberg to that of Drucker. It gave me new insights how to improve the way we manage our company."
- **Spontaneous:** the enthusiasm of the moment ensures a long-term effect.

Donna Fisher gives some good tips about the occasions for sending "thank you notes" in her book, "People Power:"

- Thanks for the support
- Thanks for your friendship
- Thanks for the introduction or referral
- Thanks for the ideas you shared with me
- Thanks for your interest in our organization
- Thanks for the encouragement
- Thanks for the opportunity to get to know your company
- Thanks for your trust in me/our organization
- Thanks for sending me the article about...
- Thanks for remembering me
- Thanks for the opportunity to do business with you
- You're one of my favorite customers. Thanks for the nice cooperation.
- Thanks for the opportunity to have a meeting
- Thanks for taking the time to...
- Thanks for staying in touch

Send a gift:

Although "thank you notes" will usually do the trick, there may be occasions that you want to do something extra, especially when someone introduced you to a new customer or a new employer and when the relationship between the two of you "allows" this.

Special gifts:

- Tickets for the other person's favorite sports event or play
- A cartoon that has a special meaning for this person or a caricature
- A book about a subject that the person is interested in
- A (framed) announcement or article about the organization the other person works for or a personal achievement
- Her favorite flowers
- A box with handwritten words of inspiration

Other gift ideas:

- Personalized Post-it notes
- A letter-opener
- A business card holder
  - For on a desk
  - For storing business cards on events
- A subscription to a magazine, eZine or website
- A plant
- A gift basket
- A fruit basket
- A calendar

- A pen or set of pens
- A CD or DVD

Some searches on the Web will give you even more inspiration!

Remember: giving a present also gives you a good feeling, especially when you took the effort to find something special or personalized!

To conclude the tips regarding thanking and "The Golden Triangle" in general I offer you a quote from (the real) Mother Theresa:

***"Kind words can be short and easy to speak,***
***but their echoes are truly endless."***

## Trust

"If there is little or no trust," says Stephen Covey, author of, "The Seven Habits of Highly Effective People," – "there is no foundation of permanent success."

In general, whom do you contact when you need advice or help? Or when do you introduce, refer or recommend someone? When there is a certain level of trust.

Have you ever met someone who had lots of opportunities for you, but who refused to share her contacts with you? Most probably this person didn't trust you or at least not at that time. Some people try to do business or get access to the network of people they meet from the first moment, and this causes reluctance by many people. Don't be one of them. Take the time to build trust.

You will encounter people who are rather reluctant to give introductions and referrals. They are very protective of their contacts. Maybe they have a good reason for that. Maybe they have been confronted with a situation of misplaced trust. It's not a good idea to force such a situation, but you don't need to give up at the first sign of protective behavior. Try to find out under which conditions they might introduce you. Discover which circumstances they feel safe to let you contact their network.

# Networking Attitude in Practice

When you want to do business with someone, work together or be introduced, this person needs to trust you. He needs to trust your expertise and the fact you are going to behave properly towards the people he introduces you to. So, how do you build trust?

## Building trust

The first step in building trust is to be appreciated by someone.

According to a survey featured by Greet Pipijn in her Starting Today course, these are the top reasons to appreciate someone:

1. comes across as friendly and polite
2. notices my presence and remembers my name
3. does everything to keep his promises
4. does everything to understand my needs and opinions
5. connected me with the person who could help me best
6. offered help, but not in an irritating way
7. was patient and helpful, listened to my story
8. reacted empathically to problems
9. treated me with respect
10. helped me, advised me to do the right things or to find what I needed
11. gave recommendations that helped me make decisions
12. spoke to me in common language, spoke my language
13. never gave me the feeling of being inferior to him/her

These are characteristics that are important in any situation, personal or professional. Appreciation is a necessary first step to build trust.

When you really want to build trust, you should know that there are two levels of trust: trust on a personal level and trust on a professional level.

## Building personal trust

To build trust on the level of your own person, you could do the following things:

- Have integrity
- Have real interest in other people
- Think – "What's in it for them?" instead of "What's in it for me?" or to put it differently: think "How can I help them?" Instead of only thinking about "How can they help me?"
- Keep promises
- Listen
- Walk your talk
- Share personal information
- Keep in touch on a regular basis
- Don't lie
- Ask good questions in order to help others to get a better picture of their situation
- Think of the Golden Triangle of networking: give, ask, thank

## Building professional (or expertise) trust

To build trust on the level of expertise (be it your work or a hobby), you could do the following things along with the things that build personal trust:

- Give examples of similar projects or cases you did in the past
- Tell success stories

- State some facts (numbers, dates, specific names, results)
- Use testimonials or references
  - Tell or show the testimonials yourself
  - Have somebody else tell them
  - Somebody else gives a testimonial without you asking for it (but this is something you have less control over)
- Mention your years of experience
- List certificates, awards, training courses and other education
- Mention a connection with well known, credible organizations or persons (but only if this is true, don't pretend to know or work with people you met only once!)
- Share professional information

In many business environments there is not only little attention for building trust on the personal, but also on the professional level.

Organizations that do pay attention to the personal level tend to organize team building events. This is a step in the right direction, but not always enough. In team building there is almost exclusively a focus on the personal level. The expertise level is almost always neglected. Why is this? Normally we don't get to choose whom we work with. Most teams are assembled by someone else (who either knows or pretends to know the expertise of the team members). However, we still have the choice regarding whom we like on a personal level and whom we have lunch with. Because the interpersonal level of liking or disliking each other can influence the atmosphere in a team, most team building exercises focus on that. That's an important aspect, but not the only one. Many people still think they have to do things on their own, and if they don't have this attitude, they frequently don't know where to go to get help. That's why it is important to share expertise in an organization, and not only about the current project or skills, but also past experiences, good and bad. A step in the right direction could be making a Networking ID for all co-workers and share these ID's with the whole organization (see also the tips about "Your networking ID" on page 94).

## Building trust through storytelling

There are more and more training courses about "storytelling" nowadays. People can learn to tell a story about an experience or how to make a metaphor of the vision of an organization. Stories are powerful, because they add a dimension to the "hard facts." They are remembered more easily. Stories appeal to the right half of the brain – hard facts to the left. If we receive information in both hemispheres, the message is reinforced and is stored better and longer.

To build trust and to appeal to both of our hemispheres, metaphors, analogies, examples, stories and more specifically success stories are the perfect medium. People will remember those stories (and you) better than a boring and vague introduction.

What are your success stories? – In your work and in your personal life. Which situation is a good example of who you really are as a person? What story do you have to show your competences and capabilities? How did you help your customers improve their situation? Make sure you have your own (success) stories!

## Shortcuts to build trust

To be trustworthy you better match the above criteria, but this takes time. However, I have good news for you. There are some "shortcuts" to build trust and/or to get introductions to other people. Here they are:

- **Act with a "Give and Receive" attitude:** offer something without expecting anything in return.
- **Specialize yourself:** if you have a specialization in the area of work or a hobby, people will be more willing to refer to you. People generally don't

believe organizations or persons who pretend to be everything for everybody. When you have a specialization, you unconsciously give the message that you don't know everything about anything. You become more human and less of a "company brochure." This appeals to people, especially when you have a nice (success) story to support this.

- **Look for common contacts:** the existing bonds of trust are levers to bring your relationship and your amount of trust to a higher level.
- **Offer an example of your expertise:** give a free sample of your product or invite someone to your seminar or training course. (You can find other ideas in the part about "Giving" on page 64).
- **Have some references:**
  - **People:** customers, partners, suppliers, and network contacts.
  - **Publications and awards:** articles or books you published, awards or certificates you received.
  - **References from common contacts are the best:** Always look for common contacts that could be perceived by the other person as good references. Remember it's not important that they are good references for you. They have to be good references for the other person.
- **Transfer trust from one situation to the other:**
  - If you are a member of the board of the local soccer team and people praise you for the work you do for the club, this trust is automatically transferred to your professional and personal situation.
  - A success story from your personal life that shows your values and capabilities is automatically transferred to your professional life. For example: a heroic act of saving a child without thinking about your own life will have a positive impact: you will at least be perceived as not being selfish. But beware: this is also true for negative things, so be careful whom you tell about your wild escapades in your town's nightlife!

Always check first which of those "shortcuts" appeal most to the person you are talking to. How do you do that? Listen to him. Really listen to him!

## Listening

One of the things I find the hardest myself is to keep asking about the changes in people's lives. To be able to understand and to "manage" the world we live in, we categorize things and people. From the moment someone belongs to a specific group or category in our mind, it is hard for them to get out there (especially because they don't know how we categorized them). It is up to you and me to get updates from our network.

The skill we need for that is "real listening" or interactive listening. Really listening to people is hard. I thought I was doing a great job myself listening to people. A few months ago I participated in a training course to improve my Emotional Intelligence, given by Greet Pipijn of "het Emotionele Intelligentie Instituut" (Flemish for the Emotional Intelligence Institute, which by the way is heavily recommended, also for "left brainers"!) One of the assignments was to gather some characteristics and areas for improvement about myself with input from friends, family, customers, suppliers, and partners.... One of my top characteristics as perceived by other people seemed to be "listening." Because I value listening very highly, I was very happy with this response.

Then I read somewhere about a simple test to know if you are really listening. In a conversation most people start to talk about their own experiences. They just listen to you to gather keywords to start their own story, and because they use some of these words they think they are doing you a favor, when in fact, in many cases, they are not on the same wavelength as you about the topic or just boring you.

The test I was talking about is this: "Hear yourself talking. If the first sentence contains the words "I" or "we" instead of "you," then the chances are high that you are not listening to the other person, but that you are building up your own monologue." Even for a good listener this is not always easy.

## Why listening is so important

Listening is the **most important skill you need to network.** Through listening you build a bond of trust. Through listening you gather information to see how you can help someone else and how you or your network can be helped.

When you really listen, people get the feeling that they really have contact with you and that you are really interested in them. The result is that they become more open and that they share more information about themselves. Then you are actually starting to build a relationship.

Because only a few people can listen well, you have a good chance to get noticed in a positive way when you really listen to people. Besides, research has pointed out that the efficiency of people to listen is only 13%, so there is much room for improvement. The tips below will help you to increase that number substantially.

Before we move on to the tips, here are two sayings I want you to think about:

- We all have two ears and only one mouth. In other words: listening is twice as important as talking.
- The things you tell people, you already know, but you might still learn something from what other people tell you.

To help you feel more comfortable, I have put the listening tips into four groups: intention, body language, actions and things you best stop doing in the future.

## Intention

Effective listening begins with a genuine desire to listen to other people. This also means forgetting about you for a minute. Often, without intending to be rude, your enthusiasm for a subject and your own desire to hear yourself talk cause you to forget courtesy. You may be so involved with your own point of view that you forget to listen to what is being said. You just stop listening!

Here are some tips that might help you:

- **Be eager to learn:** always try to learn something from the conversation.
- **Be patient:** Give the other person enough time to tell his story to you. If you don't have the amount of time necessary, communicate this and make another appointment.
- **Listen with the intention to gather information,** make a connection and create rapport (building mutual trust and affinity).
- **Look for things you have in common** to get on the same wavelength (see also the tips about "Find common ground" on page 142).
- **Be helpful:** Listen for information that signals that there is something you can help the other person with. To build a relationship it is especially recommended to listen for ways you can help someone else without a direct benefit for yourself. Of course, if you feel you have the perfect solution, you can talk about this.
- **Be empathic:** Try to look at the situation from the other person's point of view. This is not easy, because all things that happen in our lives, contribute to the way we look at the world. It is very normal to perceive the world from your own standpoint. If you are capable of abandoning your own point of view for a moment and try to understand the other person, you'll get respect and people will remember you.
- **Change your hierarchy of looking at situations:**
    1. from the point of view from the person you are listening to
    2. from the point of view of your network (how can you match the person you are listening to with your network so they can both benefit)
    3. from your own point of view

In many cases we only listen from our own point of view. You'll stand out of the crowd by not doing this and you'll also have better relationships.

## Networking Attitude in Practice

- **Understand that there are different ways and styles of communication:** You have your own style and have a preference. Don't judge people right away; give them a chance, and evaluate later. Looking for commonalities helps to get over the differences in communication styles.
- **Be sincerely interested:** in people and in what they say. People feel when you're not interested, at least at a subconscious level. Don't fake it.
- **Let go of the idea that you need to be right:** Once you and the person you are listening to both understand this, listening becomes less difficult. This frees everyone to listen rather than keep trying to convince the other of their "rightness." This tip establishes a common understanding that listening does not require people to definitively alter their opinions, beliefs, and values.
- **Watch your own emotions:** If what the other person is saying triggers an emotional response in you, be extra eager to listen carefully, with attention to the intent and full meaning of his words. When we are angry, frightened or upset, we often miss critical parts of what is being said to us.
- **Beware of disagreeing, criticizing or arguing:** Even if you disagree, let other people have their point of view. If you respond in a way that makes the other person defensive, even if you "win" the argument, you may lose something far more valuable: the relationship!
- **Be sensitive to your emotional deaf spots:** Deaf spots are words that make your mind wander. They set off a chain reaction that produces a mental barrier in your mind, which in turn inhibits the continued flow of the speaker's message. Everyone is affected by certain words so it is important to discover your own individual roadblocks and analyze why these words have such a profound effect on you.
- **Mind reacting to the message, not to the person:** Don't let your liking or disliking of the physical appearance of the other person cloud the content of his story.

- **Keep an open mind:** The other person might be saying something that you strongly disagree with, but if you allow him to finish his story without you interrupting him, you might find that his point of view is not that different from yours or you may even have learned something new.

## Body Language

Body language also plays an important role in listening. Here are some tips:

- **Turn your body to the other person.** This shows respect and interest in the other person. You "open the door" and invite him to talk freely.
- **Have an open posture.** The most important thing is that you are aware that an open and relaxed posture invites people to talk and enables you to pay closer attention. In many courses you learn not to cross your legs or arms when listening to someone. This is a sign that you are not open to the other person. You can use this as a control mechanism: crossing your arms or legs could be a good signal for you to check whether you are still giving your full attention to the other person.
- **Make eye contact frequently.** But don't exaggerate. How would you feel if somebody is staring at you the whole time? Or the opposite: a person who doesn't look you in the eye, doesn't come across as a self-confident person. Or seems to be hiding something. In any case, this is not someone you eagerly want to include in your network. Don't exclude yourself from other people's networks.
- **Have a friendly, but rather neutral facial expression** that radiates being open and unprejudiced.
- **Nod.** This doesn't mean that you nod to agree, but it shows that you're listening to what the other person is talking about.
- **Be calm.** Don't fidget; don't play with things in your hands. Playing with a pen or tapping with your foot against the table is an annoying distraction.

- **Put the other person at ease.** Allow her space and time and give "permission" to speak. Our posture and our expression make a huge difference. Relax, and let her relax as well.

My golden tip:

- **Smile.** If this seems to be too obvious for you, ask the people around you if they see you smile a lot. Most probably the answer will be "no." You don't have to be laughing loudly all the time. A gentle smile will do.

Suggestion: look in the mirror and smile at yourself. Make some variations and see what you like best. Then do it everywhere. Smile consciously at people on the bus, at work, in the supermarket. Smile at all your networking contacts. If you think this assignment is too easy for you because you already do it a lot, you should be enjoying it even more!

## Actions

***Denis Waitley: listening without bias or distraction is the greatest value you can pay another person.***

Next to having the intention to listen carefully to other people and to mind your body language, there are several other tips to improve your listening skills.

- Give your **full attention** to what is said. Don't let your thoughts wander off and don't try to think about what you are going to say next.
- **Encourage the other person** to tell you his story. Feel free to say: "Go on!"
- **Don't interrupt the other person.**
- **Listen to what is NOT being said.** Pay attention to the body language of the other person. Find out if there is a "hidden question" in a story – a question that you can give an answer to.
- **React considerately and consciously** instead of impulsively.

- **Have the other person talk more than you do yourself.** Research has revealed that when we feel really good about a conversation we just had, we were talking 80% of the time or more. If you want to be perceived as someone who is pleasant company, you don't have to tell stories and jokes all the time. Just listen and let the other person talk most of the time!
- **Ask open questions:** these are questions that begin with words like what, how, when, where... Avoid closed questions that can be answered with yes or no. Asking open questions is the way to avoid the following kind of conversation: "Hello, nice to meet you. Is this the first time you're here?" "Yes" "Do you like it here?" "Yes" "Did you have trouble with traffic?" "No" and you can go on without making progress. Instead you could have asked: "Hello, nice to meet you. How many times have you already attended this event?" "This is the first time." "What do you think thus far?" "The people are really nice and the speaker seems to be interesting." Now you have two ways to go on: "Apparently you already met some people. Who did you meet?" or "What about the topic of the speaker appeals the most to you?" Then chances are that you will have a very pleasant conversation.
- **Look at the person** you are listening to, don't look at the people behind or next to him.
- **Avoid drawing your own conclusions.** Always check them by saying, "Am I correct in assuming that...."
- **Create a positive listening environment.**
  - Ensure you get distracted as little as possible (by rumor of your colleagues or noise from the street).
  - Create an "empty space" between you and the other (step from behind your desk for example).
- **Let others tell you their own story first.** When others explain their situations, they may reveal interesting facts and valuable clues that will aid you

in helping them solve their problems or satisfy their needs. By letting them speak first, you also save time. When their interests are revealed you can tailor the rest of your discussion to their particular needs, goals, and objectives and you can avoid an inappropriate conversation.

- **Write important things down.** When you are at a networking event where you are going to meet several people, it is hard to remember everything, BUT only note keywords that help you remember the whole story. Don't try to write everything down, because when you are writing you are only hearing parts of what the other person is saying! Find your own way of dealing with this, because it's an important, but tough issue.
- **Find the emotion behind the words** (vocal and visual messages) rather than the literal meaning of the words. Ask yourself these questions when another person is speaking:
  a. What are the other person's feelings?
  b. What does he mean by what he is saying?
  c. What is his point of view?
  d. Why is he saying this?
  e. What is implied by what he says?
- **Listen for "keywords."** These are words that you have in common with the other person. More importantly, these are the words that you can use to match two people. If I hear that somebody is a Russian-French translator and I know of someone who needs someone to translate some documents with regard to exporting to Russia, then there might be a link. The keywords that triggered me were "Russia" and "translator."

My golden tip:

- **Count to three after the other person has stopped talking and before you begin talking yourself.** Often the other person continues to talk before you reached three and then the "most valuable information" is disclosed. Many times this is the moment where the real story comes to the surface. If you can control your need to tell your own stories, this will be rewarded. Even if it's not information that is useful to you, these are the moments where the relationship is strengthened.

## Stop...

In order to be a better listener, you also have to stop doing some things:

- Stop judging.
- Stop talking! It is difficult to listen and speak at the same time.
- Stop thinking you already know what's going to be said.
- Stop hanging on to your own opinion and your desire to be right.
- Stop focusing on what you are going to say next.
- Stop thinking that listening is the same as not talking.
- Stop thinking that you can't be a good listener.

I want to conclude these tips about listening with a quote from Dale Carnegie:

***"A professional networker is someone who attentively listens...***
***to a subject he knows everything about...***
***told by someone who knows nothing about it."***

# Chapter 4

# Your networking profile

Who is responsible for the web of a spider? The spider, right? Though the analogy may at first sight look a little awkward, networking looks like the activity of a spider. Like the spider, a networker is the only one who is responsible for weaving his web and maintaining it. The web of a networker is his list of contacts; the flies that a networker catches are opportunities. The larger and stronger the web, the more and better opportunities will stick to it. However, the spider analogy cannot be used 100% of the time:

- The first difference between a spider and a networker is that a spider stays alone, while real networkers connect their webs to create and attract more opportunities. Sometimes it is even necessary to join forces and have several webs connected in order to "carry the weight of a very big fly."
- The second difference is that a spider eats the flies it catches and then goes on. A good networker doesn't consume his "flies," but cares for them so they are kept vibrant and attract other "flies," other opportunities.

How do you start "weaving your own web?"

As I've already said, you have to start from the beginning, by looking at yourself. Who are you? What are your strengths? What is your "added value" to your network? What makes you special? There are more than six billion people on this planet and every one of them is unique. What makes YOU unique?

Many people have difficulty answering this last question. If you feel this way, you could start by looking at your present situation: why are YOU doing the job you do, and not somebody else? Why were YOU chosen for this project, and not one of your 100 colleagues? Why did your life partner choose YOU above all other people in the world? Why do your friends prefer YOU to hang out with? Also, think about your passion, values and goals.

Next to these more fundamental questions, other things are also important: what are your professional and personal interests? What are your hobbies? What do you enjoy doing in your spare time? What is your favorite sport?

These are all aspects of your "networking profile." Your networking profile is a description of who you are. Why do I devote a whole chapter on this? Because your networking profile represents you when you are not there yourself. The importance has increased dramatically since the rise of networking websites like LinkedIn, Ecademy, Xing and Ryze. In the "real" world it is very important that your network knows you well enough in order to spread the word about you!

What does such a networking profile look like? A networking profile consists of the following aspects:

- Your networking ID
- Your 50 words
- Your introduction
- Your Elevator Story

## Your networking ID

In my networking training courses, I do an exercise called "making your networking ID." This helps people to get to know each other better.

This exercise is also good for you for at least two reasons:

You think about yourself and are reminded of your own strengths. If you do this exercise seriously, you can (re) discover where your passion is. You get a list of things to talk about with your network contacts. You have a basis to start finding common ground.

Below you will find an example of a networking ID that I use in large companies, like Alcatel. Though the details differ from company to company, you get a feeling of what it could look like in your own organization.

First look at the networking ID and then read why these aspects are important and how to deal with them.

| | |
|---|---|
| Name: | Picture |
| Department: | |
| Telephone: | |
| Email: | |

My current function:

My current project:

My previous functions/projects/employers:

I'm looking for:

I'm offering:

My skills (things I have learned and have become good at):

My talents (qualities I was born with):

My personal hobbies/interests

- Sports:
- Hobbies:
- Books:
- Films:
- Music:
- Travel:
- Associations:
- Other:

Accomplishments from my professional or personal life that I'm proud of:

Other things people should know about me:

Let's look at the different parts of the networking ID:

- **Name, department, telephone, email:** these are the contact data that are normally available in every "company address book" or "who is who?" These are the basic data you need to get in touch with someone.
- **Picture**: most people are bad at remembering names. A visual like a photo would help them a lot – not only after, but also before a first contact. Make sure to have a recent picture so people will recognize you. A networking ID is not a beauty contest; it is an aid for your network to better remember who you are. Include a recent (!) picture, it will help improve your visibility.
- **Other data:** these are for other people to get to know you better on a professional and a personal level. They will have an idea of what your responsibilities are and what you are working on. All these data are aids for them to make a connection with you, to find commonalities and be able to help you; even without you asking for it, and this helps you to do the same for them.
    - **Current function and project:** your current professional status and function. In many cases this is a list of abbreviations. Translate this in "human" language.
    - **Previous functions/projects/employers:** your accumulated expertise. Specialization or a unique combination of varying projects can make you an invaluable asset for your organization. But how many people know that? This is the spot to tell the rest of the organization about your expertise.
    - **I'm looking for:** your wants or needs. For example, information or people you need to accomplish something. This can be professional or personal. Even within companies you should be careful about asking for "sales leads." People will first need to know you better before they

open their external network to you, even when you are working for the same organization.

- **I'm offering:** this is not about products or services, but about knowledge and contacts. Offering your specialized knowledge to others, especially if it doesn't cost you any time or money (for example a special paper or report you have written), will speed up the trust and relationship building process. For inspiration reread the chapter about the Golden Triangle.
- **My skills (things I have learned and have become good at):** this is about things you can "do." For example your degree, profession or additional courses you have taken.
- **My talents (qualities I was born with):** what makes you "attractive?" This is about the things people connect with. For example, that you are generous, kind, truthful, honest, funny, and a good listener. Make it more concrete by giving a short example. Let's assume you work as an engineer in a large R&D department where you are the (certified) wireless communication specialist (this is your skill). In this case, a talent could be that people always come to you for advice, professional and personal, because you are incredibly good at asking questions. The founder of the online network Ecademy, Penny Power, calls this part about talents "Emotional Wealth." Through Emotional Wealth you really connect with people. As a consequence, mutual beneficial relationships emerge and grow.
- **Personal hobbies/interests:** this will give other people more insight into who you really are as a person, not only as a colleague.
- **Accomplishments that you are proud of:** though this is very difficult for many people, it is recommended that you fill this in. Despite your

reluctance about "bragging" about yourself, this will show your competencies, experiences and preferences. If you stick to the facts, this is no problem. It is recommended that you write a short story about your highest accomplishments, because a story stays longer and better in people's minds. They will remember you better (and you will remember them better by their story). Another advantage of writing this small story is that this brings back memories and the great feeling you had at that moment.

- **Other things:** other things you want to share with people so they can get to know you better and find common ground.

Some recommendations about filling in your networking ID:

- **It is very important to be as specific as possible.** It is better to have only one hobby listed with a concrete example (for example, "Running the marathon of New York each year") than a list like running, soccer, watching movies and reading books. It is also important to list the things that are rather uncommon (for example, bobsleighing when you lived in Jamaica). This gives other people the opportunity to ask questions about that.

I was pleasantly surprised to hear some people at Alcatel talk about their hobbies in one of my training courses. One engineer was also a painter and the other one organized diving vacations for handicapped people. During the breaks they were the people who were asked a lot of questions. They didn't have to make the first contact anymore.

If you are a little uncomfortable with making contact with other people: have your own unique skills and interests clearly listed and look for these things in other people's IDs yourself. Trust yourself: if a specific word triggers you in any way, ask a question about it. All too many times, we hear someone talk about something and we think we already know what it is all about, but still there are some words that stand out. Don't let them go by. Ask a question, go more into detail. Help the other person tell her story.

- Use the words people use when talking about your topics of interest. Use "normal" language. This helps people to relate to you. You appear "more human." It also helps for your online networking actions. On these platforms the search functionality is very important. Use words other people might use to find you. It is, for example, better to use "plumber" than "sanitation engineer."

## 50 words

On the networking website, Ecademy (www.ecademy.com) you have a profile that looks like the one we just described. One of the parts of the profile that is rather unique is what they call "50 words." These are 50 words about you from all areas of your life. These words vary a lot from person to person. The nice thing about the Ecademy website is that you can click on these words to see who else has this particular word in his "50 words list." It's an easy way to discover people with the same interests.

Some of the people from the organization itself also put these 50 words on the backside of their business card. I thought this was a nice idea and started to do it myself too. Though some people might rather be "scared" to expose themselves like this, the reactions are usually very good. By showing your 50 words you give the opportunity to the other person to find common interests or in this case common words. You almost immediately see the change in the way the conversation goes. It is livelier, more intense and trust is built much faster.

Whether you can have these 50 words printed on your business card or not, it is a good exercise to make your own list. It gives you topics to start a conversation, to find common ground. If it's difficult for you to think of 50 words, you could involve your network. Ask them what words they associate with you. These words can be a variety of things: characteristics, values, hobbies, interests, family situation, sports, food or drinks you like, books, films, music, favorite sports team, your Myers-Briggs type (or another personality test)... Anything that contributes to your "whole picture" is good.

If you still have no inspiration, just log on to Ecademy (www.ecademy.com) and browse through the profiles. You can look, for example, at the profile of Thomas Power (chairman of Ecademy), Hendrik Deckers (chairman Ecademy Benelux) or mine. You can also look at the profile of people of your own organization or of that of partners, suppliers, customers, conculleagues, and friends...

And finally, Thomas Power, the chairman of Ecademy, advises to listen for those 50 words when you have a conversation with someone and to write them down. What you do is force yourself to really listen to someone and to ask questions to get 50 words. Those 50 words will help you remember someone. Don't forget to go for the more unique words like extreme sports, an unusual event, a special holiday, or a favorite dish in a foreign country...

## Your introduction

Your introduction is the short (seven to nine seconds) message that you tell people when you meet them and are asked what you do.

Your introduction consists of:

- Your name. Pronounced slowly! Many people complain that others do not remember their name, even if it's not a difficult one. Most of the time it is their own fault: they don't pronounce it clearly. The reason is that we are used to saying our name all the time, so for us our name is something normal, something obvious. What happens with things we find "normal?" We don't give them much attention anymore. The same happens to our name. We just "throw it out" instead of slowing our pace and pronouncing our name slowly and clearly. In networking it is important to "help others to help you." One of the ways is pronouncing your name slowly and clearly.

- Something about you, your profession or your organization that people will remember. Something that makes you stand out from the crowd. Something unique. This can be funny, but it doesn't have to be. If humor is not your strong side, it is better to avoid this. It can backfire on you.

Your introduction will also differ from situation to situation. In her book, ***"How to Work a Room,"*** Susan RoAne gives the example of John Doe, the new director of development for Memorial Hospital. He might use these variations:

- At his first meeting of the Development Director's Association, where everyone in attendance is a director of development, he might say, "I'm the money-raiser for Memorial." It's alliterative and memorable.
- At a cocktail party to introduce administrators to new board members, he would say, "I'm John Doe, your director of development."
- At his daughter's wedding, "I'm John Doe, Mary's father. Or more lightly, "I'm providing the dough for this party."

These introductions are pretty basic. It helps to include a little humor. At the introductory meeting of a non-smoking seminar, John might say something like, "I'm John Doe, and I consider myself this program's greatest challenge."

According to RoAne your self-introduction has three purposes:

1. Tell people who you are
2. Give them a pleasant experience of you
3. Give them a way to engage

A final word of advice of Susan RoAne: speak clearly and look people in the eye. Your introduction can be laced with humor and perhaps even some information that will stimulate conversation. But in the final analysis, what people will remember is the warmth and enthusiasm they feel from you.

Another book about introductions or "memory hooks" is, *"Seven Second Marketing"* by Ivan Misner. In this book you can find lots of examples of how other people introduce themselves.

An introduction is not only worthwhile to draw people's attention and to be remembered better. Many people only ask about what you do because it is part of courtesy, not because they are really interested in you. Don't spend your time and theirs by telling them a whole story. Only when they are really interested after hearing your introduction, do you move on to your "Elevator Story."

## Your Elevator Story

What is an Elevator Story? It is a short story about yourself you can tell people in 30 seconds so they get an idea of what you do, who you are and/or what added value you can bring. The name "Elevator Story" is derived from the time frame between getting in an elevator at ground level and leaving it on the eighth floor.

What it comes down to is that you have a story that appeals to the people you meet. In the first place it has to get them interested in going more into details and asking more questions. This can be on the spot or at a later moment in time. Secondly, your Elevator Story needs to serve as a "vocal" business card, so people can tell their network about you in the way you want them to.

Other names for the Elevator Story are: elevator pitch, sales pitch, introductory speech, 30 second speech, two minute drill...Personally, I don't like most of these "labels." For me they have the connotation of being self-centered (or even remind me of hard sellers), while in networking the focus should be on the other person. Although the Elevator Story is also a story about yourself or the organization you represent, this is more a means to create a bridge between you and the other person than a tool to persuade someone.

## Why is this Elevator Story so important?

Remember the 6 degrees of proximity? Everybody has an average 250 direct contacts. In second degree we have 31,250 contacts, but we can't tell our Elevator Story to those 31,250 people ourselves. Our direct contacts should be able to "represent" us when they are talking with their direct contacts. This means they should be able to tell them your Elevator Story almost as well as you do.

Crafting a good Elevator Story is not easy. In fact, it's almost impossible. Why? Because every situation is different. There is no one-size-fits-all Elevator Story. You have to be creative to adapt your Elevator Story to your specific situation.

"If my Elevator Story is different every time, what's the use of preparing it?" you might ask.

Most people I have met have never even given a second thought about their Elevator Story. By taking the time to think about one and draft it, is sometimes enough to have the necessary ingredients and enough self-confidence to improvise at all future occasions.

In my experience it is also very powerful to sit down with all people involved and narrow down an Elevator Story for your organization, your department or your team. In sales teams this is a very good exercise. The sales representatives learn from each other how they talk about the organization and how they present themselves. This not only inspires the participants and boosts their self-confidence, but they also get to know each other better. Because of the positive act of working towards a joint goal (the Elevator Story) this is a simple team building exercise with great results!

## So what does an Elevator Story looks like?

I make the distinction between an Elevator Story for your organization, department or team on the one hand, and a personal one for you on the other hand.

## *Elevator Story for your organization or department*

For an Elevator Story for your organization or department you could use these ingredients and even this structure:

- For whom... (target group)
- What, which need is satisfied (offer)
- Unlike, other than, different from, contrary to... (positioning)
- Name product, service, organization, department, person ("label" of the offer)
- Benefits (no features!) for the customer (customer experience)
- Your knowledge, contacts...(added value to the network)

Be concrete, specific and practical. Use facts, no claims!

An example of an Elevator Story for your organization or department is that of Intuit Quicken. This example comes from the book, *"Crossing the Chasm"* by Geoffrey Moore:

"For the bill paying member of the family, who also uses a home PC, who is tired of filling out the same old checks month after month, Quicken is a PC home finance program that automatically creates and tracks all your check writing. Unlike "Managing Your Money," a financial analysis package, we have assembled an entire system just for home bill-paying."

What can we learn from this Elevator Story?

- You can't be everything to everyone. People don't believe this. Quicken focuses on the "bill paying member of the family who also uses a home PC." This is not for companies, not for kids, but for the bill paying member.
- There is a "problem:" "filling out the same old checks month after month." Many people from the target group will recognize this and be eager to listen to the rest of the story. People who don't belong to the target group

probably know someone with this problem, so they could be interested to pass this information on to their network contacts.

- A description of the product and the solution for the problem: "a home finance program" (again not for companies) "that automatically creates and tracks all your check writing." This solves the problem of doing this by hand month after month. There are no detailed features how they do it, only the benefit is stated: "automatically."
- The most important part is positioning: "unlike "Managing Your Money," a financial analysis package, we have assembled an entire system just for home bill-paying."
  - There is a comparison with something people know. It is always much easier to understand and to remember something when we can compare it to something we already know. This is especially true for new companies, products or services.
  - It is a positive statement: nothing bad is said about the other package. Only the differentiation: financial analysis versus an entire system.
  - Again "home bill-paying" is repeated: this way it sticks in people's minds.

## *Personal Elevator Story*

For a personal Elevator Story you could use these ingredients:

- What are your strengths and skills?
- What benefits can others reap from cooperating with you?
- What is your passion?
- What is your expertise? Not only with regard to your current job, but also the previous ones and specific knowledge concerning your hobbies, sports or other interests.

- Which degrees do you have? Where did you study? Did you receive any special certificates or awards?
- What's your current function, what was your last function or what did you like best up until now? And why?
- Which organizations did you work for? Paid or as a volunteer.
- What makes you different? What difference do you make? And how do you do it?
- What's your added value to the network?
- How does what you do help others?
- Other things that are special or noteworthy about you or your situation.

If you are looking for a new job, you will benefit from creating your personal Elevator Story.

An example of a personal Elevator Story is:

"My name is Frank Jones. That is Jones, like the rock singer. I worked for 16 years for several IT companies as a project leader for conversion projects. This means for that we ensure that none of the data is lost when new software is installed. I worked on projects for companies like Johnson & Johnson, IBM and Coca Cola. Like Tom Jones I was always able to keep the team in good spirits despite deadlines and tight budgets. For example: when it was New Year's Eve 1999, we were responsible for a Year 2000 conversion. Against all expectations, we finished the project three days before the deadline. Though everything was checked and double-checked, none of the team members got off. We all had to be at the premises of the customer. You can imagine that this was a disappointment for most of us. Then I came up with the idea of a karaoke party in the restaurant of the customer. Although the party was without alcohol, it was one of the best New Year's Eve parties ever!"

What can we learn from this Elevator Story?

- He makes the link with Tom Jones. Most people know Tom Jones and subconsciously make the link between Tom Jones and Frank. He increases his chances to be remembered the next time. If you do this, make sure you pick someone people know. One of the participants in a training course for BMW, Glenn Mylle, always refers to the connection with Glenn Miller.

  The minor disadvantage that he has is that a lot of people don't know Glenn Miller. More than once people have called his office and asked for "the guy with the name like a singer." Although his method doesn't work 100% of the time, people remember him and in the end that's what matters.

- He gives facts and figures: 16 years of experience and names of customers: Johnson & Johnson, IBM, Coca Cola. People are more or less familiar with these names. This builds trust.

- "Keep the team in good spirits despite deadlines and tight budgets:" although this is not very concrete, people can imagine the situation. Most of us know that it's not easy to keep everybody happy. Frank also stands out from the crowd with this statement. Most people would rather talk about budgets, deadlines or technical aspects of projects. By not doing this, Frank makes a positive impression.

- The story:

  - Using a story ensures that he will be remembered. When you were reading the story, you made pictures in your mind. You imagined a restaurant, a karaoke machine with one or two microphones, maybe a small stage, you saw fruit juice and soda (and maybe you felt sorry for them not having an alcoholic drink on New Year's Eve), you saw people singing, dancing and having fun in this unusual setting...These are all pictures you store in your mind.

- The phrase "I came up with an idea" and the actual realization of the idea shows that he has leadership abilities. "Three days before the deadline" adds even more to the positive impression. It shows that Frank is the kind of man who can make things happen.
- "Although the party was without alcohol, it was one of the best New Year's Eve parties ever:" this is a man who can enjoy himself without alcohol. This also contributes to his reliability.

## *Pitfalls when drafting an Elevator Story*

When making your Elevator Story, watch out for these potential mistakes:

- Making it too long. You don't need to use all ingredients! Stick to 30 seconds. You can always elaborate when people start asking questions.
- Terms only used in your industry. This is sometimes a real plague, especially in the software world. Avoid abbreviations or explain them. If you do start explaining them, remember you only have 30 seconds!
- Focus on yourself instead of on the (internal) customer. Many organizations only talk about themselves, not about the benefits of their customer. I once offered a website marketing scan. From the 86 websites I scanned, only two were not entirely focused on the company itself, but on their customers. It is quite normal that you are focused on what you are doing on a daily basis and that you look at the world from your point of view (or from your organization's point of view). Since this is normal human behavior, empathy, the art of looking at the world through somebody else's glasses, is so important in networking. NOT being focused on your own situation makes you stand out from the crowd.
- Using features instead of benefits. This is probably the most common mistake we make when introducing ourselves to other people. We talk about

the features and expect the other person to automatically derive the benefits. This is especially true, when you represent a high tech company and/or the other person is not that technical, chances are that he stops listening after 10 seconds. Even if you are aware that you have to explain the benefits, failing to do so in the first few moments and talking about the features first instead, will cause him to stop listening.

For example: "We use the Microsoft.net technology to build websites. We have four people who are certified Microsoft programmers, so we are the best party to build your new website."

How does this appeal to you? How many stories like this have you already heard?

Now for the most confronting part: have you already looked in the mirror and honestly looked at your own presentation? Does it look like the example?

An alternative for the above example could be: "Most organizations want a website that looks good, is stable and reliable and is based on technology the IT department is familiar with. We invested in training four people in the latest Microsoft technology (called.net). This technology allows fast and reliable implementation, while using the same platform as before. In practice this means that a website can be up and running within three weeks without any efforts from the customer's IT department."

## *"Don'ts" when using an Elevator Story*

Avoid these things when using your Elevator Story:

- Writing the Elevator Story down, memorizing it and using it again and again "without thinking." People like people, and they want to talk to people, not to robots.

- Meeting people and immediately begin by telling them your Elevator Story. Wait until you are asked for your introduction. If they are interested, you can move on to your Elevator Story. I recommend you ask the other person to tell his story first. Listening and asking questions is not only a better way to build a relationship, but it also gives you a better insight in what ingredients you should use for your own Elevator Story. The best Elevator Story is the one that suits the person you are talking to best. How do you know that? By listening to the other person first!
- Using negative words. Using words like "There are only three employees in our company," "We are struggling to survive" or "We are just new in the market and still finding our way, without much success until now." This doesn't make a good impression. You don't come across as very trustworthy, on a personal and/or company level. Always speak in positive terms about yourself and the organization you represent.
- Using only a general Elevator Story:
  - One that applies for the whole company, but is not adapted to the specific situation of the person you are talking to or the particular event you are attending.
  - One consisting only of claims or vague words. For example: "We offer fast delivery, high quality and a good price." This applies to every company (or at least, I hope so). What makes yours different? Give concrete examples and use facts and figures.

    An alternative for the previously mentioned example could be: "We deliver within three working days, which is twice as fast as the average delivery time in our industry. This allows our customers to have three extra days to make modifications or reduce their time to market by three days."

## *Tests to evaluate your Elevator Story*

Drafting a good Elevator Story is not easy. Here are some tests that will help you.

- "Grandmother test" for "listener-friendliness:" tell your Elevator Story to your grandmother (if she is still alive, an elderly neighbor will do, too) and ask her to tell it back to you. Then you will notice which words to keep and which to replace.
- "Conculleague test" for appeal: replace the name of your organization, product or service by that of a conculleague. If the Elevator Story still makes sense, then it is too vague. Work on what makes your organization special. Work on the positioning.
- "Not test" for vagueness: This test is to make sure that your Elevator Story is not too vague. That it doesn't only contain claims. If we take the example: "We offer fast delivery, high quality and a good price" then the "not test" results in: "We don't offer fast delivery, high quality and a good price." This makes no sense and thus fails to pass the "not test." It is too vague. It is only a claim. If we apply the "not test" to the other example: "We don't deliver within three working days" then this makes sense, because the average delivery time is six working days. Nobody expects you to deliver in three, so this example passes the test, meaning it's not too vague. Use numbers and concrete examples!

# A final word about your networking profile

When I do the "Elevator Story" exercise in my training courses, there are always participants who say: "Such an Elevator Story is not natural and besides before I get to 30 seconds, most of the time I was already interrupted by someone asking me a question." They are absolutely right. That's what happens in most of the cases when you are enthusiastic and especially if the person you are talking to is a good networker.

Let me repeat the value of the exercise of crafting an Elevator Story:

- Having an Elevator Story or at least a basis to start from, gives many people the small bit of confidence they otherwise lack to initialize contact with other people.
- The focus on the benefits for the other person, and more importantly for the other person's network, will ensure more and better questions. It will also make other people remember you longer and increase the chance that they will pass your story on to their network (and in the way you wanted).

Another comment I regularly receive in the context of the networking profile is: this "networking ID" looks like a CV (Curriculum Vitae) or resume. That's true, but there is a difference. The difference is that you make a CV to "sell" yourself. The networking ID is designed to find common ground and to help you and your (potential) network to help each other. So, even more than in CV, it is important to be honest. It's the only way you can make a real connection, build trust and help each other in a meaningful way.

Even if you are reading this book without participating in a training course or without your organization being interested in networking, it is a good exercise for you to do. You will feel more certain about yourself at the next networking event. You can use the topics from the list to start or maintain a conversation, so make sure that you fill in your networking ID.

# Chapter 5

# Networking at events

Most people associate the word "networking" with meeting people at receptions, fairs, conferences, trade shows, parties, meetings and other (networking) events. Maybe you thought that this book was only about this aspect of networking, or maybe this was the chapter you were primarily looking for. Whatever the case, I have good news for you: in this chapter you'll get lots of tips about networking at an event.

## A Networking Story

*Eric is outside the building of a networking event where he's never been before. He's nervous, his breath is irregular and the palms of his hands are sweaty. "Go on" he says to himself. "You can do it." He enters the building and gets his nametag, constantly thinking: "What can I say to them? How do I make the first contact? Will there be any interesting people? Maybe attending was not such a good idea. I still have lots of real work to do, and my wife is complaining that we don't see each other enough."*

*He takes a deep breath and enters the room. He sees no one familiar. "This is going to be a tough night," he says to himself. Then he walks to the bar to order a drink. Other people enter. Eric is still at the bar, waiting for someone to start a conversation. But no one comes. The other people are talking to each other. "Oh no," he thinks. "They all know each other. How will I ever get in contact with one of them?" And time ticks away. "I give it another half hour," he says to himself and orders another drink. Other people also order drinks. From behind a brochure he found at a table, Eric is peeking at them. "That one looks very important. He probably doesn't want to talk to me. The woman next to him seems nice. I hope she notices me and starts a conversation. Oh no, another woman recognized her and is now talking to her. Who is going to come to talk to me?" Half an hour later, Eric leaves the event. Disappointed again. "Networking events are not my cup of tea. I'll tell my boss tomorrow that he should go himself next time."*

Do you recognize (parts of) this story? Maybe not all of the symptoms are familiar to you, but you probably recognize the situation. Don't worry; this is rather normal. Several studies were carried out to discover what the biggest fear of people is. There is still discussion about what number one is: speaking in public or meeting a room full of strangers. In any case, both beat dying when it comes to the biggest fear. If you ask me what the biggest fear is, it would probably be a combination of the two biggest fears: speaking in public to a room full of strangers. If you belong to a networking club where it is the custom that you present yourself in front of all other members, this could indeed be a frightening experience.

Maybe you are already a loyal member of a networking club and don't share Eric's feelings (anymore). Maybe you feel more like Nancy in the following story:

*Nancy is a regular of networking club "Connection." She's already been a member for seven years. Every time she attends a meeting, she is happy to see the five other women she got to know at the first event she attended. Every meeting they have so much to tell each other that the evenings are over before they know it. It is always great fun and also good for business. They help each other with information about suppliers, partnerships and new laws. The saleswomen among them even offer each other sales leads and make introductions. So, all goes well. Or not? Last time Nancy really began to wonder if it's such a good idea to stay in her small group. Who are all those other members? What are their stories? In fact, she is very curious to have a talk with them, but she doesn't have the guts to share this with her small group. They took care of her and are always there for her. They are so loving and caring, on a business level as well as on a personal level. Going to talk with others feels like betraying her friends. What to do?*

## Attending an event

Before we get to the practical tips and help Eric and Nancy out, I would like to remind you of our mental thresholds or barriers. Even our biggest fears are imaginary most of the time. If you fear attending networking events, it might be a good idea to reread the part about "The attitude" on page 23 before continuing.

Attending an event consists of more than just being there. These are the steps you have to take to get the most out of a networking event:

1. Preparation
2. Entering the venue
3. Making contact
4. Maintaining the conversation
5. Ending the conversation
6. Leaving the venue
7. Follow up

The first six steps will be covered in this chapter. You can read more about step seven "Follow up," in a separate chapter because follow up doesn't only apply to networking events.

### Preparation

The saying: "Good preparation is half the battle" applies to attending networking events, too. But what does this mean in practice?

There are several topics to consider when preparing for a networking event:

1. How do you know that an event is organized?

2. Which networking event to attend? And which not?
3. What does the event look like?
4. Who are the other attendees?
5. What is my specific objective at this event?
6. Do I have my tools?
7. How do I feel when going to a networking event?

## *How do you know that an event is organized?*

The answer might sound quite simple to you, but I'm still surprised how many people don't know that there are events that are very interesting to them.

It starts with knowing your goals. If you know them, it is easy to find out what's being organized and where to meet people.

If you have to start from scratch (meaning you are not a member of any organization yet), these are my recommendations:

- **Share your goals with your network and ask which organizations could be interesting.**
- **Use search engines** like Google on the Internet with keywords that are linked to your goal to find organizations you might consider joining.
- **Find out who are the major players (people or organizations) in your industry or field of interest.** Ask them which organizations they are a member of, and which they recommend. Also, ask why. The best situation is that you can contact someone from your current network. If you don't know anybody, don't worry. First ask your network if they know anyone. If you still haven't got a name, just pick up the phone and make a call.

  This telephone call is also a great substitute for a cold sales call. You are not selling anything, just asking for help. In the meanwhile you are building a relationship. Don't sell during this same conversation, especially if it's a contact you received via your network. Don't sell unless the other party insists. You must beware that you don't ruin a relationship before it even starts!

Once you obtain some names of organizations. The next steps are:

- Visit the website of the organization you found.
- Check who is already member and contact them. Tell them you are interested in becoming a member. Ask them what they like about the organization and the events and what they don't like. Ask for other organizations they are a member of and which they recommend. The same comment applies to the major players in the tip about starting from scratch.
- Contact the president or chairman of the organization and ask why you should join. Ask what the benefits of a potential membership are for you. Ask if you can get an invitation to try the organization out before becoming a member, and before paying large membership fees.
- Subscribe to newsletters of the selected organizations. This way you never miss an event. You can always check out the calendar in the specialized magazines.
- Keep asking your network and the people you meet at events which other events they recommend. Also, ask why. This way you will learn a lot. Not only about the organizations and events, but also about what's going on in your field of interest and about the people you meet. You will have more interesting conversations. As a consequence, your relationships will be strengthened and your network will grow both in quantity as in quality.

It's obvious that the importance of the organizations and their events vary from person to person. In general, I want to advise you to consider joining one or more of the following organizations. If you join one of every type, most of the networks are covered.

- **Your industry organization.** This is what I call a "vertical organization." This organization unites all the companies of a specific industry or sector, like telecom or automotive.

- **Your professional organization.** This is a "horizontal organization"– like the association for marketers or accountants. For this kind of organization it doesn't matter which industry you are active in, as long as you have the specific profession they represent.

- **A local networking organization.** The local Chamber of Commerce or a service club like: Lions, Kiwanis or Rotary.

- **Your alumni organization.** The bonds of people who studied at the same university or (high) school are amazingly strong. It is no secret that many politicians in the United States studied at the same university and even were members of the same fraternity or student union. They help each other out because of their common connection with the university, even when they never met in person before.

- A special category is **online networking organizations** like Ecademy, Xing, LinkedIn, Ryze and many others. Because of their new and special nature a large part of the next chapter is dedicated to them.

All of these organizations can be local and global. Of course, it depends on your situation and your interests, but it is always good to have local connections. You never know what might happen to you in the future, and then you will be happy to have a local network as a safety net.

If you are in between jobs or are looking for another job, then you should consider attending events of the industry and professional organization that are related to the job you want.

## *Which networking events to attend?*

We all have busy lives – you, me, and all our other networking contacts, so it is important to use our time intelligently. This means giving thought to which networking events to attend and which not.

The most important question to make a good decision is: what is your goal? This time it is about your goal at the event.

Is your goal meeting prospects, maintaining the relationship with your customers, sharing information, learning new stuff, looking for a new supplier or a new co-worker, finding other people or organizations to team up with or just meeting other people?

You see that there are several goals. They can be different from event to event, and they can depend on your function within your organization or role at the event.

It is also very important to be aware of the fact that your goals can be different from those of the other people at an event. For example: a freelancer or a one man or one woman company lacks the social contacts that people working for large corporations have. Their goal at an event could just be socializing with other business people. They could be just looking for someone to talk to, not for customers, suppliers or partnerships.

Another example of different goals is that of an organization of Human Resource

Managers. Until 2002, they only allowed HR managers. No one else could become member. The focus of the meetings of this organization is information and experience sharing. In 2002, HR consultants were also allowed. The conditions of their membership were rather strict. They had to sign an ethical code that they were not going to sell to the HR Managers. Although this could avoid some of the possible conflicts between the goals of HR Managers and consultants, it is a good example of different and even conflicting goals.

In this example, it is made very clear that selling is not wanted and probably won't happen. But is it also that clear for other events? When it comes to yourself: when you are planning to go to an event, do you stop for a moment and think about the fact that the other participants might have other goals than you?

Be aware of your own goals and those of others and it will be much easier to decide which events to attend and which not.

### *What does the event look like?*

Prepare yourself further by finding an answer to the following questions:

- What's the type of the event? Is there a speaker? Is there time to network? How much and when? Do you have to present yourself to the whole group?
- What's the format? Is the event a dinner, or a breakfast meeting? Or are there just some snacks, the so-called finger-food?
- What is the dress code? There is nothing more embarrassing than to show up underdressed. Being overdressed is better, although this can give you an uncomfortable feeling as well. When you show up in your new cocktail dress and the others are wearing jeans, you don't seem to fit in the occasion. Avoid this by preparing yourself. If it's not clear from the invitation, ask the organization. They are only a phone call away.

### *Who are the other attendees?*

You are going to a networking event to meet other people. Do you know who is going to be there? What is the "profile" of the other attendees? Are they the people you want to meet? If you want to meet the technical people from your sector and only sales people show up, you might consider attending another event.

Do you have the **list of participants** a few days before the event? When I ask this question in my training course, people tell me: "Most of the time I don't receive one." When I then ask them if they took the time to ask for it, 80% admit they don't make the request. Many organizations don't provide the list because they don't have the necessary resources or the right technology. Many organizers are also volunteers with time constraints, but when you ask for the list, they will probably send it to you.

Another issue with lists is that some organizations want to protect the privacy of the attendees. As a consequence, they don't want to distribute all the confidential data like email addresses and personal phone numbers – and they're right! Personally, I'm not interested in those data. I'm only interested in the names of the attendees and the name of the organization they represent, and if possible also the function.

You don't need more data to prepare yourself. Remember you are still in the preparation phase. The real connection has to take place at the event. Ask the organization for only the names of the companies and their representatives at the event. Few organizations will deny this request, especially if you explain to them that it makes no sense for you to have the confidential contact data. If you didn't get to meet a person and you send her an email or call her out of the blue, what impression does this make?

How would you react if someone emailed or called you without ever meeting you? This is almost always perceived as SPAM. In other words, this backfires on you. So, why should you do it? If you explain this to the organizer of the event, they will give you the list.

One of the things I like about the "offline events" of the networking organization Ecademy (www.ecademy.com) is that the built-in registration software automatically makes an attendees list for you. You can't only see who is coming and read their profile on the website, you also have a printable overview. On this overview you find the practical details like date, time, location and program. More interestingly, all names, pictures and names of the organizations the attendees work for are printed, too. This makes it very easy to prepare for an event and to make contact with each other at the event and before.

Now, suppose you have the list in advance. What do you do with it? Do you only look at the names of the companies and of the names of the attendees? Or do you use the list as a preparation tool?

You could use the list to help you prepare for the event in the following way:

- Use the Internet to do a search using the name of the company – preferably on news sites. This will give you something to talk about.
- Visit the website of the company that interests you.
- "Google" the person you would like to meet. This means that you search on the name of this person in Google. You might find some very interesting facts that you can use in your conversation. The person you want to meet might have given a presentation on an important conference two months ago. Or he might have won an award. Or he might be the coach of a soccer team of 12-year olds that took home the cup last year.

If you took the time to prepare on the attendees, you don't only feel more comfortable and ready, but you will make a very good impression. Almost no one prepares properly for an event. Just by doing this, you will stand out from the crowd. You also give the message that you are interested in the other person. Everybody is flattered when they receive genuine attention (although not everybody will show this). You will also come across as well prepared and not superficial. This stimulates trust and strengthens the relationship.

## *What is your specific objective at an event?*

We already looked at the importance of goals at an event. The specific objective is even more detailed. If your goal is to find companies to set up a partnership with, your specific objective at the event could be: "Tonight I want to meet three companies that are candidates for a partnership." Making this more specific will help you to focus more.

In order to reach your specific objective more easily, you can share it with the other attendees. Chances are that they will think of your objective when talking to other people. They can serve as a sort of ambassador. If you never shared your objectives before, try it. It will not only help you reach them faster, but you will always have something to talk about.

Be an excellent networker and also ask others what their objectives are for the event and in what way you can help them to reach them.

## *Do you have your tools?*

Tools? Yes, your networking tools. They are:

- **Business cards.** Never go to an event without them. Read also the part about "Business Cards" (on page 166).
- **A pen.** To make notes on the back of the business cards or on a separate piece of paper if you brought that with you. Please do make notes. If you talk to 15 people at an event, it is hard to remember what the first conversation was about and which actions you promised to undertake (or what the other person was going to do for you). Make notes so you can remember this person. Most of us have trouble with remembering names, so be sure to take notes.
- **The nametag.** Most of the time the organization provides you with a nametag. Here are some tips to use it wisely:
  - Wear it on your right side. At most of the events I visit, people wear the nametag on the left side. When shaking hands both people have to reach out to read the name of the other person, because their bodies are turned away from each other. When the nametag is on the right side, this is no problem.

- **It is OK to read the names of other people.** But taking a sneak peek doesn't leave a good impression. It's not the reading of the name that causes an occasional negative reaction it is the sneakiness. Personally, I need to read the name to be able to remember it better, so I definitely and obviously look at the nametag while saying "Excuse me, I like to read your nametag so I can remember your name." Notice my intention. I clearly say I want to remember them (and I really mean it!) Nobody ever gave me a strange look for doing this, because they felt it was my genuine intention. I suggest you follow my example, in deed and in intention!

- **Bring your own nametag.** Though this is a tricky one. It has advantages and disadvantages. It is something that can help you when the organization doesn't provide nametags. Since many people need nametags to remember names, you can help them to remember you by wearing your own nametag. However, some people will perceive you as arrogant and a showoff when you are the only one wearing a nametag. So, apply this tip wisely.

• **Conversation starters.**

- I once read the story of a man who deliberately **turned his nametag upside down**. People came up to him and told him about his nametag being upside down. He thanked them for their kind remark, turned the nametag and started a conversation. When the conversation ended and the other person went away, he turned his nametag upside down again. For him it was a great conversation starter. People came to him, so he didn't have to approach them. If you're still shy, this could be a tip for you. But one remark: I still wonder what he does when he bumps into someone he already met.

- Susan RoAne, the author of "How to Work a Room" and other networking books, always wears an eye-catching **broche.** In "How to Work a Room" she mentions that Madeleine Albright, the first female Secretary of State of the United States of America, does the same.

- For men Susan RoAne gives the tip to wear a **specific tie**. However, my own experience tells me to be careful with this. Sometimes it is hard to tell whether it is done on purpose to have a conversation starter whether it is a testimonial of someone's bad taste. In case people are confused, they would rather not talk about it, not wanting to embarrass the other person, and they silently chalk it down to bad taste. So, be careful!

• **Subjects to talk about.**

- Read the daily newspapers or news websites.

- Inform yourself about the latest developments in the (professional) fields of interest of the attendees at the meeting.

- Sports are almost always a good conversation starter with men.

- As an organizer you can make sure that there are conversation starters. The company Elan Events, for example, organizes the event "Femme Totale." This is an event for women only. One of the "conversation starters" the organization provides is a fashion show during dinner. Whether the clothes appeal to the audience or not, they are the topic of conversation.

• **Marketing material other than your business cards.** Normally it is not appropriate to take brochures or other marketing material with you. The reason is that this looks too much like selling and people don't want to walk around with a bunch of papers. A possible alternative is that you provide a small checklist or "tips from the expert." It's important that you don't sell, but help people. The size of this marketing material should not exceed the size of the left inner pocket of a man's suit, so he can put it away. Women normally carry a purse where they can store their material.

- **Things people can remember you by.** At networking events there are usually lots of people. You meet them only for a short period of time. Help people to remember you. You can do this via your conversation starters, the subjects you bring up in conversation, your business card, other marketing material and your clothing and grooming. In general, I suggest you do at least two things:
  - Find one physical thing people can remember you by.
  - Really listen to people. If you succeed, they won't forget you. Use the tips about "Listening" on page 94.

## *How do you feel when going to a networking event?*

I have some advice for you that you might find rather surprising: if you really have an aversion to the event you are supposed to attend, don't go. Simply don't go, because it will be a failure. It is a kind of self-fulfilling prophecy. If you expect it to be boring or a waste of time, that is exactly what it will turn into. You will radiate your negative feelings. As a result the interesting people will stay away from you and you will only attract the people who feel like complaining or who are boring.

It also works the other way around. You can also attract the right people by having a positive attitude. When you believe in yourself and are proud of who you are and what/who you represent, people will tap into this.

Something that helps you get in this positive mood is doing a visualization before you leave for the event. You can do it in the car (but mind the traffic!) or before you enter the venue. Picture yourself speaking with enthusiasm and talking to interesting people. See yourself being capable of listening to people and giving them your full attention. Imagine that they are grateful for your courteous behavior and that they introduce you to other people. Visualize the event as being fun and interesting.

By doing this exercise you get in the mood, and you will find that the event really will be fun and interesting.

Two very practical tips to sharpen your positive attitude: look people in the eye and smile! You don't have to laugh, but do smile. Mean it. Most people can "feel" when a smile is fake. You can also see it. Daniel Pink illustrates the difference in, "A Whole New Mind." It is in the eyes. When someone smiles genuinely, the outer muscles of the eyes contract. Most of us feel it when a person fakes a smile, but now you know what to look for.

Going to a networking event with a positive attitude will make a huge difference!

### *Bring your networking partner?*

If you are still feeling uncomfortable about going to a networking event despite the previous tips, you might consider not going alone, so you have someone to fall back on. But beware. Going with a friend, colleague or partner has several potential dangers:

- **Talk to each other all the time.** I see this very often with people who work for the same company. They are having a great time, but just by themselves. A networking event is not the right place for an intimate party. It is the place to get to know other people and to maintain existing relationships. If you really want to enjoy yourself, there are much better places. Having a party only with colleagues at a networking event is a waste of time, and a potential danger for the reputation of the organization you work for. You and your organization might get the reputation of being "asocial" and not reliable. Avoid this.

- **Turn off other people.** It's easier to step up to a person who is alone. By walking around together you create a barrier for others. You are less approachable.

- **Leave the event early.** If you brought someone who is not familiar with the event and/or is bored after half an hour, you could be tempted to leave the event and be unsatisfied yourself.

  Carefully choose whom to invite to go with you. Also, be careful when accepting invitations to accompany someone else to an event.

Don't get me wrong; attending a networking event together with an acquaintance has advantages too. Given that you both go your own way:

- **You both have your personal PR agency.** In two ways:
  - If you're not in the direct vicinity, your networking partner could distribute your business cards.
  - If you are nearby, it is even better. Then she can introduce you to the other person, and she will do that much better than you do it yourself. She will emphasize your strong points and the benefits for other people. Most people have difficulty with self-promotion. The ones who don't are usually perceived as arrogant. A (business) friend who praises you is the perfect solution!

- **You both meet people that you can introduce each other to.** When you split up, the two of you can meet more people than on your own. The chances that you meet someone who is really interesting for you increase substantially. Moreover, when you have met a person who is interesting for your networking partner, you can introduce them to each other. You strengthen your relationship with both of them.

- You have your **"life saver for boring and seemingly never ending" conversations.** Sometimes you get stuck with someone who is not that interesting (anymore). Although I suggest you end the conversation yourself in a nice and decent way, your networking partner could be your hero of the night by coming to your rescue. A perfect phrase for your networking partner in these circumstances could be, "I'm sorry to interrupt your conversation, but I wanted to introduce you to someone I just met." In order to be each other's "life saver," it is a good idea to have a secret signal (a gesture or a specific phrase).
- **It's easier to approach groups.** It's not always easy to approach a group when you are on your own. At least that is the perception of many people. When you do decide to walk around together, this is the moment to approach groups.
- **You know that there is someone to talk to if all other people are not interested in you or not interesting for you.** In practice this would never happen (the only exception might be that you didn't prepare for the event), but it gives a sense of security and comfort. As a consequence, you might feel better and more open, and like we already saw, a positive attitude makes a big difference.

## Entering the venue

When do you start networking at an event? Most participants start networking when they enter the room where the actual event is taking place. This is a pity. Why? – they missed a lot of opportunities.

Let's go over some of those opportunities in a special way: in reverse order. Picture a movie that you rewind.

- **Reception desk:** here you get lots of opportunities:

- While waiting for your nametag, you can start a conversation with the people in front or behind you.
- Ask for the attendance list (if you didn't get it beforehand): if you didn't plan how to deal with the event, this is your last chance for preparation.
- My golden tip: connect with the organizer. If she is not there, ask the host to point her out. Always thank the organizer for her efforts to organize the event and the invitation. Do this sincerely. No sucking-up allowed. People feel when a compliment is not real.

- **Lobby:** if it is a large venue, the lobby could be the place to start a conversation with potential co-attendees. If the people you approached are not participating in the event, at least you had the opportunity to work on your "contact making" skills, and maybe you had a nice and fruitful conversation, too.
- **Parking:** the same as with the lobby. Use your time from the parking lot to the reception area efficiently and effectively by connecting with other people.
- **A few hours before the event:** meet another attendee for breakfast, lunch or dinner before the networking event starts. This is a perfect opportunity to have a one-on-one chat and to optimize your travel time (avoiding traffic jams, having other meetings…).
- **A few days before the event:** you can contact other attendees to invite them for breakfast, lunch or dinner. You can also have a small private meeting before or during the event, or you can ask to talk for five minutes during the reception. Making this physical contact at the event (or only on the phone) makes a follow up afterwards much easier.

The advantages of connecting with people before entering the room itself are multiple:

- **They are not in groups yet.** Lots of people come to an event alone. They probably know people who are already inside the room or who are still coming. It is easier to make contact with people who are alone. This is more likely to happen in the moments before entering a room.
- **They are not focused yet on people they want to meet.** Most people who did their homework have a list of people they want to meet. They start looking for them from the moment they enter the room. Unless you or your organization is famous, you won't be on this list. Connecting with them before entering the room gives you the opportunity to speak with them before they are occupied in other conversations.
- **You get in the networking mood.** You could consider these conversations as a warming up for the rest of the event.
- **Maybe you will find a networking partner for the rest of the event.** If you didn't bring a networking partner to the event, but you're still more comfortable with having one, this might be the moment to find one.

## Making contact

The most dreaded thing in networking for most people is making contact with other people. What about you? How do you do it? If you need some help, you will find some practical tips in the next sections.

Remember: making contact starts with your attitude and the way you think of yourself. If you think you're not worth talking to, people will feel this and indeed not talk to you. However, as you know, everybody has something interesting to say and to offer. (If you don't remember what this could be for you, you can reread the tips about "Giving" on page 64).

## *Find common ground*

"OK, I understand that it is important to find commonalities. But what do I have in common with other people at an event where I have never been before?" you might ask.

There are always at least three things you have in common:

- the physical location
- the event and its theme and/or program
- the organization

Other things you can talk about are their relationship with the organizer, their names, the company they work for, their job, the place where they work or live, hobbies and other interests...

If you look at this list there is a lot to talk about. It's **not only what you talk about with people, but it is also about how you start or continue a conversation.** Your questions have to be good. One of my golden tips is: **"What aspect of your job do you like most?"**

Why is this a good question? It is an open question and a question that can be answered by anyone. Nowadays, unfortunately, many people are not happy with their work, but there are always aspects they find interesting. Give them the opportunity to talk in a positive way about their company (or department) and about themselves.

It also gives you lots of options for your next questions. For example: the other person might answer: "I like the variety and the contact with people." Then you can ask "Tell me more about this variety, what do you do specifically?" or "What kind of contacts do you have, how do you cooperate with people?" or "Can you give me an example of what this means in practice?" Examples and stories are great because you can remember them better.

## *Conversation starters*

In my training courses people always ask me for conversation starters or the so-called icebreakers. I strongly recommend that you don't really prepare your openers, but talk to people spontaneously. However, I still want to give you a head start, so here are some suggestions.

Topics:

- Physical location
- Event and its theme and/or program
- Organization
- Name of the other person
- Name and/or activity of the organization the other person represents
- Job or function
- Town where the other person works or lives
- Hobbies and other interests
- General news
- Sports
- Developments in the field of interest of the organization of the event or of the person you are talking to

At business events it is OK to use clichés. It is less a turn off than in a bar or nightclub, so you can talk about the weather or about the traffic. The most important thing is that you get the conversation started, but I hope you will make the effort and think about some other original and interesting openers. It is also better for your reputation if you are able to ask good questions, people will remember you better.

It is not only important what you say, but how you say it. I will give you some examples of sentences you might use. Of course, some of the questions are easier in one situation than another. Let them inspire you to make your own!

Open questions:

- What in the program appealed to you?
- Who do you know in the organization?
- How well do you know the other attendees?
- What aspect of your job do you like the most?
- Who invited you?
- Where did you hear of this event?
- What activities is your organization involved in?
- What makes your organization special? What makes your organization unique or different than others?
- Where does your name come from? Does it have a special meaning?
- Where do you come from?
- Besides your work, what are your other interests?
- What's your opinion on the latest technology breakthrough in our industry?
- How do you feel about meeting other people at networking events?
- What's your favorite sport?

Closed questions (are best followed by an open question):

- "Are you a member of the organization?"
  - Answer = Yes: "For how long?" or "What do you like best about the organization?"

  - Answer = No: "Are you planning to become a member?" "Why (not)?" "Which requirements do you have when considering joining an organization?"
- "Is this your first time at this location/event/this year/...?"
  - Yes: "What are your expectations?" "Who do you like to meet?" "Who can I introduce you to?"
  - No: "What are the differences with other times?"
- "Did you watch the game of the national soccer team yesterday?"
  - Yes: "What would you have done if you were the national coach?" (almost every sports fan has an opinion about how to play)
  - No: "Do you like soccer and sports?" or "What's your favorite sport?"

My golden tip is to begin your question with: "How do you feel about...?" This is a very safe question. You don't ask the other person about his opinion. When a person has to state his opinion, he would like to give the best possible answer after considering the pro's and cons. He has to be careful about what he is going to say and how he is going to formulate it. A question about a feeling is less "threatening": "It is only a feeling". But you get the best possible reply, because people tend to decide emotionally (feelings) and explain their decision rationally. If you get a "feeling response" you know that this is something that really affects someone. This is a good basis to really connect with another person, beyond the usual business or superficial talk.

***Denis Waitley: If you must speak, ask a question.***

## *Look for people who are alone*

Now you know that you have to look for common ground and have prepared some conversation starters. So, whom do you address first? If you are still a bit unsure, look for "wallflowers:" people who seem to be glued to the wall and take no initiative to meet other people. This may sound negative, but when you remember the barriers we talked about, it is very normal that some people behave like this.

If you sometimes feel a bit like a wallflower yourself, it is even better to approach them. It is not only easier to approach someone who is alone, but you will also score "bonus points." This means: by approaching them you did something they didn't dare to do. They will respect you for that. They will be grateful for "saving" them, and maybe you'll find yourself a networking partner for the rest of the event. If you need a self-confidence booster, go talk to wallflowers.

### *Go to the bar or food area*

If you've attended a networking event, you've probably noticed that the atmosphere in the surroundings of the bar or the tables with food is different. People are more relaxed. This is a good place to start a conversation.

Note: food and drinks are always a good conversation starter. A word of warning: only give comments about the food when they are positive. Negative comments damage your reputation with other people, especially when you just met them seconds before.

The same applies to humor. It is great when you are funny, but don't make jokes at the expense of other people, or don't tell subversive jokes. Do you remember the last event when an attendee was telling dirty jokes and making obscene remarks about other people? People may have laughed and he may have thought that he was popular, but did you call him to do business with or did you contact him for other "serious" matters? Probably not. Why? He didn't build trust with you. Actually, he subconsciously gave the message: "I'm doing things behind people's back. Not only at events, but all the time, and this will also happen when doing business with you." Don't get caught in this trap yourself and avoid subversive humor.

## *Play host (ess)*

What do you do when you are throwing a birthday party and you are the host of the evening? You welcome people, you make them feel comfortable, you provide them with drinks and food and you introduce them to each other. You don't wait for them to ask you for something, but you take an active approach. You focus on the well being of others – not your own. It makes you feel great by doing this.

Just as Donna Fisher advices in, *"Professional Networking for Dummies,"* I also recommend that you do the same at networking events, even when you are not the organizer. What you can do is radiate a "host (ess) attitude". If you focus on playing an active role at the event, people will be grateful. You will have fun, be appreciated and feel valuable.

Play the host (ess) at the next event by doing the following:

- **Greet people.** Even if you don't talk with them, nod and give them a genuine smile.
- **Make people feel comfortable.** Give them your full attention and listen to their stories.
- **Get them something to drink or eat.** Do this yourself or call the waiter.
- **Connect them with other people** by introducing them in a way that is compelling for both of them.

## *Help the organization*

If you still find it difficult to make contact, despite the previous tips, you might feel more comfortable by using an indirect approach. By helping the organization, for example. Let me explain why this is a good way to get in touch with people and how to do it.

The board and members of many organizations are volunteers. They are always short of money to organize things and people to help before, during and after the event.

If you read this you might begin to wonder why people want to be in the organizational committee anyway, but it has lots of advantages. The first is visibility to the other members and appreciation. Another important aspect is the transfer of trust. When they do a good job as (board) member, people will automatically transfer this image to their business or personal life.

Let me give you the example of a man who worked for the Chamber of Commerce in a region of Belgium. Though he was not a volunteer, but an employee, he benefited from being part of the organization of many events. During the period he worked for the Chamber of Commerce he met many people. He had no problems reaching them. The name "Chamber of Commerce" opens many doors. The same applies to the names of other organizations, especially when they represent a specific industry, profession or local business. For many people this man was the "practical face" of the Chamber of Commerce. He was the one who helped them at events, organized receptions and introduced them to other people. This high visibility helped him later on. After he left the Chamber of Commerce, this man founded five highly successful businesses in a row, just with the help of the contacts from his Chamber of Commerce time.

It is definitely recommended that you become an active member or member of the board of the organizations you prefer. You will learn a lot, have fun and meet lots of interesting people.

But let's assume that you are not an active member yet and that you are rather shy or feel uncomfortable at events. What can you do?

You could offer to help the organization. You can help behind the scenes or play a more visible role. Setting up the stage and microphones is more a back office job, while distributing nametags gives you more visibility. Whatever job you choose, the most important thing is that you helped the organization. You helped the most visible and appreciated people of the event, the organizers. They will be grateful for your help, and they will want to do something in return. They will be more open to your requests. They might, for example, introduce you to Mr. Big Shot. However, don't help the organization with the expectation this will happen (immediately). If you offer to help, you must enjoy helping them. Don't be calculating. Remember "Give and Receive:" give without expecting anything in return.

## *Have yourself introduced*

This is my number one golden tip for making contact with other people: have yourself introduced. It sounds so logical, but very few people use this "tactic."

Why is having yourself introduced so powerful? Someone else will tell your Elevator Story for you, so you don't have to do it yourself. Other people will always be very positive about you (something that doesn't always comes natural for you when you had a bad day). In many cases, they will also exaggerate or brag about you, and that's OK. It's their words, not yours. If you think they overdid it, you can always mention that to the other person. In any case, you begin with a head start. You begin your conversation and your relationship at a "higher level." Instead of making a "cold contact," you have a "warm" or even a "hot contact".

The most comfortable way to make the initial contact is to get introduced by someone else. Who could this person be?

- **Someone you already knew before the event:** a customer, supplier, partner, friend…A customer is the best. He is considered to be the most objective.
- **Someone you just met at the event.** Share your goals for the event with the people you meet. Chances are that when they meet someone that's interesting for you, they will introduce you.

- A very powerful, but often neglected one: **the organization.** As you already read in the previous tip, the organizers are the best known and most connected people at the event. Ask them to introduce you. They will be happy to do it; it is part of their job as hosts. However, many organizers don't have a natural tendency to do this, because they are occupied with the logistic part. If you want them to introduce you, it's your responsibility to take the initiative. Ask them to do this for you!

To get the most out of introductions, you have to help others to introduce you in the best possible way. Tell them your Elevator Story. Tell them some of your accomplishments. Keep them up-to-date with your success stories. Again, help them to help you.

Don't forget to do the same for them: listen to their Elevator Story, spread the word for them and introduce them to other people.

### *Approaching groups*

You already read that one solution to approach groups is to go with a networking partner. The advantage is a "mental" one. You both know that you have someone to talk to if the other conversations don't work out. You have a backup.

But what do you do when you are alone? How do you approach groups when you are on your own?

Personally, I have a motto in networking: "Why make it difficult when it can be easy?" When it comes down to approaching groups this means that I won't approach a group that has "closed body language." Not only individuals, but also groups have a specific body language. A "closed" group body language looks like this: four people facing each other, with their backs to the rest of the room, leaning towards each other on a cocktail table, not interested in what's going on around them and clearly having a conversation among themselves. When I see a group like this, I don't bother to go over there. They are not interested in anyone else – at least for the moment. Be patient and wait till the group opens up. If you know one of the people at the table, you can always go over and say hello, or you can have yourself introduced by the organization or a network contact of yours that knows one of them. But even in these situations, it will be hard to get their attention. Why? They are interested in each other, not in someone else. Remember though, it is only for this moment. Wait till later, the group will open up.

When the group has opened up, how do you approach it when you are alone?

These are the steps you can take:

- Make eye contact with one of them. (if the group is "closed," this will be almost impossible). If the group is ready for another member, you will notice it by how the other person looks back.
- Listen to the conversation in the group. You can ask the person who gave you "permission" to enter the group what they are talking about. Don't start distributing your business cards, collecting business cards from others or taking over the conversation with your own story. How do you feel when someone else does this? Don't start introducing yourself right away, unless you are asked to do this.
- If the conversation reaches a point where you can add a meaningful contribution, it is time to speak up. Do this without bragging or speaking loudly. This way you can make a smooth entrance in the group.

## *How to make yourself popular without spending money. Networking, the Dutch way.*

At most networking events the attendance fee also covers drinks, snacks and food. You can use this to your advantage.

- When you are waiting at the bar to order something, also order something for the people behind you. This way you make yourself popular. Not because you are paying for the drinks (it's included in the attendance fee, so they pay for the drinks, too), but because you were so thoughtful. You are not only making yourself popular, but also have the opportunity to start a nice conversation while you are waiting for the drinks.

- An alternative is when you are in a group. At most receptions there are waiters with platters full of drinks or snacks. If you step out of the circle and have the waiter come to your group, the other people will be grateful. This is not because you are paying for the drinks or snacks, but because of your thoughtfulness.

This will have a positive impact both on a conscious and subconscious level. So, do it at the next reception. It's free and fun!

## *Talk to speakers*

Speakers are not invited to give a presentation by coincidence. They are the experts. If they weren't, it would not be them on stage, but somebody else. Experts are always good to know to update your knowledge. More importantly, in the context of this book: they are most likely people with a large and interesting network and because of their expertise they are invited by several organizations. They probably know the presidents or chair (wo)men. They have customers, suppliers and partnerships, too. They also attend meetings and conferences themselves. Their status as a speaker makes it more likely that they have contacts with the so-called "higher profiles." To have them in your network and be welcomed in theirs is definitely a recommendation. So, talk to them.

Many people say to me: "Who am I to talk to this expert speaker?"

Let me tell you a little secret about speakers. They are asked by many organizations they don't really know. They speak at events they never would have visited if they weren't invited to give a presentation. Not that they are not interested, but they also have only 24 hours per day.

As a consequence, lots of speakers feel a little uncomfortable once they get off stage. Many organizers are so busy with the practical details of the event instead of talking to the speakers, that many speakers feel left alone. Many of them have the same feelings as Eric in the example at the beginning of this chapter. Although some of them are (or have become) good networkers and feel at ease, lots of them still have the same issues at starting, maintaining and ending a conversation.

The next time you are at an event where there is a speaker, talk to her. She will be a great asset for your network. Make sure that you are perceived as a valuable contact, too. Remember "Give and Receive." Maybe the only thing you have to offer is some minutes of your time or an introduction to someone else. That's OK; maybe you will have made the difference just by doing this.

A caution about approaching speakers: don't become a "celebrity stalker." If she has no time for you, don't push it. There are still other people in the room that are also interesting. Another variant of "celebrity stalking" is focusing on Mr. Big Shot who is in the room. Chances are that he is difficult to approach, and chances are even higher that you are not the only one wanting to talk to him. If you are so focused on this one person, you might miss other interesting contacts. If you are talking to them, but constantly looking over their shoulder to see if Mr. Big Shot has ended his conversation, you might jeopardize your existing relationships. How would you feel if somebody did this to you?

"OK" you might say. "But I really want to talk to Mr. Big Shot. What do I do?"

The answer is quite simple: have yourself introduced via a common contact or via the organizer of the event. Make clear to the person who is going to introduce you what you have to offer to this person and what you would like to get. Especially when a "celebrity" or "Big Shot" is involved, people are very protective about their contacts. The only way to "have them open the gate" is to show them that it is beneficial for the "celebrity" (and preferably also for the one who is going to introduce you).

## Maintaining the conversation

You followed one or more tips to make contact and are now engaged in a conversation with someone. A frequently asked question is: how do you keep the conversation going?

The most important tip is: listen! (If you forgot the most important aspects of listening, you can reread the part about "Listening" on page 85).

Listening involves an active role from your side. Asking questions is a major part of it. You can use the same questions as in making contact. For maintaining the conversation you can also use other questions, especially with the follow up in mind.

Sentences you might use to maintain the conversation, other than the ones for making contact:

- How can I introduce you best to others?
- What makes you or your organization different from others?
- How can I remember you best?
- What do I have to tell my network about you or your organization?
- How do you want me to remember you?
- What do you want me to remember you for?

My golden tip for maintaining a conversation is the question: "How do you mean?" or "What do you mean specifically?" It's a question you can almost always ask. It is a question to delve deeper and deeper into the details. It gives you lots of information.

What you are trying to do in the conversation is:

- **Find more common ground.**

- **Discover how you can help each other.** Preferably how you can be of service to the other person. This will give you the opportunity to strengthen the relationship after the event, and give you some input for a follow up action.
- **Find connections with other people from your network.** It is important to listen for "keywords." These keywords are words that remind you of someone in your network. If the person you are talking to is looking for an accountant and you have an accountant in your network, you can introduce them to each other. If you hear that someone's hobby is running marathons and a friend of yours is looking for training schemes to run a marathon: connect them.

When the conversation really doesn't work out, another solution is to **involve other people.** Ask their opinion about something that was just said. This "new blood" might give the conversation the spark it missed before.

If it really doesn't work between the two of you, just end the conversation. It is not necessary to have the same lively conversation with every (wo)man you meet. There are enough other people to talk to – for you and for the other person.

## Ending the conversation

When do you end a conversation? How long should a conversation last? And how do you end a conversation?

### *How long should a conversation last?*

As a general rule most books about networking say that a conversation at a networking event should last between five and ten minutes. Many of the people in my training courses think this is rather short. Let me explain why such a short time frame is considered the standard rule.

At a networking event the purpose is to meet new people and to maintain existing contacts. These are the moments to keep in touch and to discover if the other person might be interesting to have a "real talk" with. When you meet someone interesting, make an appointment to meet each other at another time.

Networking events usually don't provide the ideal environment for a good and deep conversation. There is a lot of noise, you don't have a seat, there is not much light, waiters are "disturbing" your conversation with drinks and/or food and there are lots of other people that want to meet you or the person you are talking to.

As a general rule you could say: "To make the most of your evening you should meet as many people as possible without jeopardizing the quality of the conversation." In practice this means a conversation of five to ten minutes.

Of course, you can only do this in five to ten minutes when both of you are prepared, know your Elevator Story and are able to ask good questions. You can't expect this from other people, but at least you can do your part.

Sometimes people say: "I only want to talk to three people that interest me and I want to spend an hour with each of them. I don't want to talk to all those other people." My answer to this remark is: this is your choice. If you want this, that's fine by me, but also think of the others: do the people you want to spend an hour with also want to spend an hour with YOU at this moment? They are probably there to meet several people, not only you. Be careful claiming people and claiming their time. Always check if that's OK for them. Otherwise, you might end your relationship before it's even started.

## *How do you end a conversation?*

Sometimes you want to end a conversation because you both want to meet other people. Other times you want to end it because the other person is boring or because you have already been talking for 40 minutes and you still want to see other people before the event is over. What do you do with the "living bear trap" that won't let you go?

Almost as many people find it difficult to end a conversation as to start one, so here are some tips to help you.

- Don't leave quietly. Don't disappear when the other person turns his head. This gives a bad feeling. End the conversation properly.
- Some people use the excuse, "Excuse me, I have to go to the bathroom." In my opinion this is a lame excuse. You run the "risk" that the other person says: "I'll join you." My advice is: do it differently.
- Thank the other person for the conversation and exchange business cards. Commit to what you promised. Ask the other person when he is going to do what he promised you (if he made a promise). In order to have the possibility to end the conversation like this, it is important to have listened well to the needs of the other person, and to have written down an action point for yourself. Otherwise there is little use in exchanging business cards.
- State why you are both here: to meet other people. Just tell the other person "We are here at a networking event, so let's both make the most of this evening and meet other people." Notice that I used the word "both." It is important to show the benefit for the other person as well.
- A variation on the previous one: tell the other person you promised other people to meet them. Remind her that a networking event offers an opportunity to meet many people.
- If you are there with a networking partner, you can call her to the rescue. Let her tell you that somebody else wants to meet you. Then you say goodbye to the other person. You can use one of the other options to conclude or just say: "It was nice to meet you. Have a great evening/morning/ afternoon/..."

- My golden tip for ending a conversation is: introduce this person to somebody else at the event. If you really listen to people you will have discovered common interests with another participant. You will do both a favor. This way you will strengthen your relationship with both of them, even if it's someone who is not interesting for you. That doesn't mean he can't get along with other people. One exception: if the person you are talking to is a real nuisance or is drunk, don't "drop" him with other people. Your relationship with those other people will suffer. In this case, you best inform the organization of the situation. Normally they, as organizers, have enough authority to handle the situation.

## *Getting out of your own small group*

If we think back of the story of Nancy who is kind of stuck with her small group and wants to meet other people, what could we advise her? Nancy could point out to her friends that the power of networking is partially to be found in a very close group like theirs. The other part is in meeting new people, getting new ideas, discovering new opportunities and learning new things.

They could be each other's networking partners and best PR representatives. They could help each other to meet more interesting contacts. They could meet each other before the event starts and have their own "mini pre event." This leaves them the time to network with other people at the event itself.

Or she could come earlier herself, meet some of the other attendees who don't belong to her small group and introduce some of the group members to them (and the other way around).

As long as she focuses on the benefits of all involved parties, there won't be a problem. She doesn't have to have the feeling of "betraying" her group. She is helping them out even more.

If you're in a situation like Nancy's, try these tips. Your business friends will be grateful!

## Leaving the venue

When you leave the event, don't forget to thank the organization. This strengthens your bond with them, and you probably stand out from the crowd, because only a small number of the attendees at events do this.

## How to stimulate networking at your event

At many events first-time attendees suffer from "fear of cold water." They really don't feel comfortable making contact with others. Another phenomenon is that the "veterans" always stick together and have trouble getting out of their group of familiar people.

I see few organizations doing anything about this. That's a pity. There are several ways to deal with it and to stimulate networking at their event.

### *Tell people that networking is important*

You can hire somebody to do it in your place at your next conference.

A conference is a special kind of networking event, because most of the time there is a strong emphasis on the topics of the speakers. Does this mean that the speakers are the most important people at a conference?

In my opinion, the real added value at conferences is the contacts, more than the speakers. Yes, you can learn from them, but most of the time their timeslot is so limited that you only get some general ideas. Many of the speakers have also written books or give training courses or offer consulting. They have rather high visibility and are easy to find if you need them, but you might never have the opportunity again to meet the attendee on your left or in front of you!

As a solution for this issue I'm frequently hired to give keynote presentations at conferences. My favorite is the one I do together with Jan De Boeck where we not only stress the importance of networking and give practical tips about how to do it, but also get the attendees to talk to each other. Since we give them the excuse to talk to each other, they tend to forget about their mental barriers. Then they discover that the other attendees can be valuable contacts. They realize that some of their fellow attendees are sometimes even greater experts than the ones on stage. At an event in the Netherlands I heard someone say during a break: "Those two crazy Belgians said that I have to talk to other people at this conference, so here I am." I love it when people use us as an excuse to make contact. When they overcome their fears and start talking to each other, I then consider my mission accomplished!

## *Use a networking concept*

When you are responsible for organizing a networking event, it is your duty to make your guests as comfortable as possible. However, what I see in practice is that most organizations leave the participants to their own devices.

Most of the time the organizers are glad that the logistics (location, food, drinks, invitations, staff...) are provided for, and who are we to blame them? Most of them are volunteers. Volunteers who are most of the time not even thanked for the effort they put into organizing the event.

But as an organizer you could do more. Welcoming people, introducing the attendees to each other and making them feel at ease are the more obvious ones. Next to this there are several networking concepts that you can use. These networking concepts make it easier for first-timers to make contact, and for regulars to break out of their familiar circles.

Some examples of concepts are Speed Networking, Network Auction and Meet and Greet. All those concepts have in common that just by helping people and being helped by other people (even by people you never met before) a very positive atmosphere is created. As a consequence, "contact making fears" melt away, as snow does in the sun.

*Speed Networking*

There are different variations of this concept, but the core is that you have several one-on-one meetings during a short amount of time. For example, in Belgium there is the Speed Business Dating (www.speedbusinessdating.be) concept where you sit down to have a five-minute talk with another person. After those five minutes, you indicate whether you see opportunities to do business or not and then move on to the next person. You have ten such talks in one session. Afterwards all participants get an overview of the matches of this session. On July 15th 2005 they had 1,096 participants in all sessions with 37.7% matches and another 15.8% where only one party saw a potential business opportunity. Amazing what taking the time for each other in only five minutes can do!

Other organizations in this area are Speednetworking LTD (www.speednetworking.org) and Speednetworking.com (www.speednetworking.com).

*Network Auction*

A network auction is a concept where requests of the participants are auctioned. The other participants hear the question and if they can help this person or know someone who can help him they "bid." The purpose is not to have one highest bid, but as many as possible. The matches are recorded and presented to the participants. The result is not only an answer to the question of the participants, but also a change in the atmosphere. People feel very grateful to have answers to their questions, they realize the enormous amount of opportunities and forget their fear of making contact!

When I am asked to do a network auction, I always suggest combining it with a small presentation about what networking is all about and with the "Meet and Greet" concept to have even better results.

*Meet and Greet*

This is a concept that I saw at various meetings, but I heard the name for the first time at a meeting of Managers for Managers, a Belgian networking club (www.m-4-m.com).

When people arrive at the event, they get a piece of paper with two numbers. The first number is the number of the table; the second number indicates the order in which people can present themselves to the other people. Number one is always for an "ambassador" who explains the concept to the new attendees and who keeps the time. Everyone gets three minutes to introduce himself to the other people at his table. This way shy people receive enough attention. At one table there are an average of eight people, so at least you hear the Elevator Story of seven people and they listen to yours. This is another way of getting in touch with people that you otherwise wouldn't have talked to. Several nice opportunities have already come out of this kind of meetings!

What's also important in the concept of Managers for Managers is that there are no chairs. People stand at their table. After the presentation round at their table they have the time to move around to meet people from other tables. Sitting on chairs would prevent this.

Let this example inspire you to stimulate networking at your next event! Or even better attend one of the meetings of these organizations or hire them to assist you to implement this concept at your event.

## Etiquette

When attending networking events some people are nervous not because they have to make contact or end a conversation, but because they don't know how to behave. They don't know networking etiquette.

The most important thing about etiquette is be yourself and have a good networking attitude (what I call the "Give and Receive" attitude). Sounds simple, but in practice this isn't always the case. All too often, fear of the unknown, insecurity or the belief that we "must" meet interesting people and establish fantastic contacts, prevent us from being ourselves and giving without expecting anything back.

Next to this basic attitude you might benefit from some extra tips about etiquette at a networking event:

- **Eat before attending an event.** Of course, this depends on the format of the event and whether or not you have the opportunity to eat something beforehand. Why this advice?
    - In the first place because the snacks that are served are not always that nutritious. Chicken wings, meatballs, cheese rolls, salted peanuts... are not the healthiest things to eat, especially when you go to two or three networking events in a week.
    - But more importantly there is another reason. Picture yourself at an event, a drink in one hand, and a shrimp salad sandwich in the other, your briefcase or purse wrapped around your body in some way or the other. Then there he comes, Mr. Big Shot, the man you always wanted to meet, but your mouth is full and in your desperate search to find a napkin, the law of Murphy strikes again: the shrimp salad sandwich (which is most of the time open on one side) slips out of your hand and makes a perfect landing on your new tie. Now you're not only dirty, but also too embarrassed to shake hands with Mr. Big Shot, providing your little performance didn't scare him away.

    In case you don't believe this could happen to you, there is another reason. Without a snack you always have a free hand to shake hands with other people or to exchange business cards and to write down keywords.
- **Hold your drink in your left hand.** When I ask the participants of my training courses why this is a good habit, they invariably answer: "To be able

to shake hands with your right hand." That is correct, but only partially. What most of us do, is hold the glass in our right hand and when we want to shake hands, we just switch the glass from our right to our left hand. So, why hold your glass in the left hand? Glasses usually contain cold drinks. Many of those drinks are also "sticky" when spilled, even if it's just a little drop, and your hands get wet from condensation or at least feel cold when you shake hands with someone. This first touch is not very pleasant (and if you have "sticky" or wet hands this could even be embarrassing).

- **Shake hands.** A solution for the previous problem is not to shake hands. By the way, in some cultures there are other rituals of greeting (see for example the article, "Shake Hands in 10 Different Languages" on the Profit Guide website: www.profitguide.com). But in general, in business environments it is the custom to shake hands. This custom goes back to the medieval ages when they opened their hands to show that they were unarmed. Nowadays making contact on the physical level is still important to build and maintain a relationship.

  As a consequence, it is also important how you shake hands. How do you feel when somebody "drops you a soft hand?" How do you react when someone thinks your hand is an orange to be squeezed as hard and as swiftly as possible? As usual the "truth" lies in the middle: give a firm, solid handshake.

  Some people give a handshake with two hands. This can also be done, but rather for people you already know rather than people you meet for the first time. Subconsciously, a two-hand handshake gives the message: "I appreciate you, I want to take care of you." If you don't know the person yet, this can't be sincere (yet).

- **Avoid kissing people, unless you are really sure they are OK with it and it is appropriate in that specific environment.** Many people find it inappropriate to kiss in a business environment and especially when they have never met you before. You better avoid the situation of the son of a Belgian diplomat who got arrested in the Middle East after kissing a Belgian lady he knew on the cheek. Thanks to diplomatic intervention he was released from jail, but he is not allowed to enter the country again, ever!

- **Address the other person the way he or she prefers.** Nowadays it is more and more accepted that you address people by their first name. Not everybody is OK with that. Remember networking and establishing a relationship is in the first place about the other person, so adapt to her preferences. How do you know? Most of the time you can derive it from the way she addresses you. If you really can't figure it out, you can always ask how the other person likes to be addressed. Maybe she is very proud of being a doctor and prefers to be addressed in that way.

- **Respect the time.** Time is very democratic. Everybody gets the same amount every day. You can't save it and you can't buy it. You have to be very careful how to spend it, and the same applies for the people you meet. Remember: if you decide to spend the whole event with one person, then that's your choice. Always check if the other person is also OK with that. Respecting time not only applies to events, but also to telephone conversations, emails, instant messaging and all other times you communicate with people. It is a good habit to indicate how much time you want from your contact and to check if she is OK with that.

- **Set your boundaries and respect those of others.** This means that you don't have to say "yes" to all the questions you receive (see the tip about "Getting requests: the power of saying "no" on page 73). If you stumble on a "no," respect it. Depending on the situation and the emotional state of the other person, you can ask one more question like "What needs to be different for you to say "yes?""

- **Turn off your mobile phone.** Avoid all other things that can distract you from establishing and maintaining relationships.

When you combine the tips concerning etiquette with all other tips about networking at an event, you definitely will be more comfortable at the next networking event, and as a consequence you will be more successful!

## Business Cards

One of the cheapest marketing tools that are available, but also one of the most neglected, is the business card.

### The importance of a business card

I still can't believe that many organizations only have business cards for their "external profiles" like sales people, managing directors, project leaders or marketing managers.

What managers who cut costs by saving on business cards apparently don't understand, is that the power of networking works for every co-worker in their department or organization.

Even more important is the fact that if you don't have a business card, you have an extra obstacle to overcome.

For many people this not only entails a practical disadvantage, but also a psychological one. The thought "I'm not important enough to have a business card" can prohibit people from establishing contact with others. Most often the people who don't get business cards are back-office employees. They tend to be more introverted than others, which gives them the feeling of having a disadvantage over more extraverted people (which is, in fact, not the case). The result is that when they meet other people in a meeting, at a reception or another networking event, inside or outside the organization, they don't even tend to network.

What beautiful opportunities are missed in this way! And besides, how vane or disrespectful to label people as "less important." You also never know who they know! Maybe their neighbor is the customer your sales representatives have been after for months, or they might have a brother that would be the perfect software programmer for your next big project. Perhaps their son plays on the same soccer team as the president of a potential business partner.

Also, within the organization this could be important: they might be very well connected with people from other departments or local offices. Many Social (or Organizational) Network Analyses have disclosed that the organizational chart is almost NEVER the way people work together, exchange information or influence each other. A very good book in this field is "The Hidden Power of Social Organizations," by Rob Cross and Andrew Parker. It is very practical and includes many case studies and examples from real business life.

Giving your co-workers business cards encourages them to represent your organization to the outside world. Once I got the answer: "That's exactly the reason why we don't give business cards to our cleaning staff. We don't want people to identify them with our company. They are not loyal and sometimes speak ill of our organization." When I heard this, I seriously wondered about how important people were in this organization. Business is still done between people, not between machines. Many large contracts are signed, not because the offer was the best, but because of the human aspect of the relationship between customer and supplier. When I hear someone say they don't believe in their own people, then I seriously doubt ever becoming a customer of this company. How will they treat me? A good beginning for this man could just be to give business cards to his cleaning staff. They might feel more respected and start behaving differently and more positively.

## Free business cards

If you are in between jobs or if you work part-time for another organization, especially your own, make sure you have business cards. If you can't afford them, visit the website of Vistaprint (www.vistaprint.com). On this website you can get business cards for free. Via the website you choose a design, add your text and then have them printed and sent to you by the postal service. The only "disadvantage" is that on the back of the card the address of the website is printed (in a small font).

However, be careful when you use free business cards to represent your own or somebody else's business. You don't make a professional impression with people that know that these are free cards. (Un) consciously, they may think: if they are not willing to spend any money on business cards, they might cut costs on their service to me, too. For a small fee you can get the same cards without the publicity on them. It is wise to make this small investment.

Now, why would a company give away these cards for free? In my opinion, it is a smart business move and one you can learn something from. I see several good reasons to do this:

1. To get prospects: people who tried the free ones are serious candidates to place an order without www.vistaprint.com on the back.
2. During the process of making your business card you have the option to upload your own picture or logo. You also have the option not to have the publicity printed on the back. For these options you have to pay. This is a nice example of upselling and in this case making some money without expecting it.
3. Another form of publicity: by passing on business cards people use the actual product and maybe talk about it. This is much better and cheaper than major advertisement campaigns.
4. Free publicity via other means, like in this book. Because I think this service is a great tip for you and my other readers, I gladly write and talk about it.

For Vistaprint this is their "low cost, high perceived value" item. It is also only one of their products besides brochures, postcards, labels, magnets and holiday and greeting cards. Let this example inspire you!

## What on a business card?

Chances are that you are not responsible for your own business card or there is a company policy about business cards. Then it might be a good idea to have the person who is responsible read the following tips, because with a little investment you might improve one of your best marketing tools.

Here are some tips about what to put on your business card:

- Is it obvious what your organization does just by its name? No? Then it is absolutely recommended to add an extra line. For example:
    - London Bike Rental
    - Company ABC– Bike Rental in the London Area.
- **Be sure to include your website and email address.** These days a business card without a website and email address is perceived as very unprofessional. If you work for a small company or have a company on your own: get your own domain name and email address that refers to your business instead of to a free Hotmail, Yahoo, AOL or local service provider account. At www.godaddy.com, for example, you already have your own domain for $8.95 a year!
- Be sure the **font is big enough** to be read by anybody, especially by older people or people with bad eyesight.
- A tough one is the **mobile telephone number.** Should it be on the business card or not?
    - One tactic is to not include it on the business card, but write it down

when you give your business card. This makes the other person feel more important (because you don't give your mobile number to everybody) and the chances that he keeps your business card increase.

- The other tactic is to include it on the business card. This avoids forgetting to provide your mobile number. It also gives the impression: "it's our company policy to always be available for you."
- Which tactic you choose, it always comes down to how you communicate it!

• Another tough one is whether or not to **use both sides of your business card** to provide extra information or a call to action.

  - Pro: you don't always have the time to talk about your organization.

    The back of the card can give extra information or attract prospects to your shop or website. Always be sure to tell people what you expect them to do. For example: "Come to our store for a half-hour demonstration of product X" or "Visit our website to get your free 'Don't Forget this on your Wedding Day Checklist.'
  - Con: there is no room left for the recipient of your business card to make additional notes about you.
  - My advice: because few people really make notes, I prefer using both sides of the card. On the back of my card I have an invitation to get your free networking eCourse on my website www.networking-coach.com.

• Put your **"50 words"** on the back of your card (see also the tips about "50 words" on page 109).

• If some of the contact data on your business card changes, order new ones. Don't start striking through old phone numbers or email addresses. For many of the people you meet for the first time, this is a complete turn-off!

- If you render personal services, you should consider putting **your photo** on your business card. This applies for instance to trainers, consultants, presenters, speakers...Your picture will also help other people to remember you. If you choose to include your photo, please select a good and representative one. Mind the contrast, light and use a recent picture. People should recognize you when they meet you again!

- Keep your business cards simple. Use only one, or maximum two different fonts. Avoid a mix of **bold**, italic and underline and different font sizes. This not only applies to your business cards, but to all your marketing material: folders, letters, websites, blogs, email, direct mail...

- **Have your cards printed by a professional printer.** You never can get a decent business card out of your printer at home. Digital printers are usually cheaper than offset. They are not that expensive and are able to print small batches. It is relatively cheaper to order 1,000 business cards than 500.

- About the **size of your business card.** On the one hand special sizes make your business card stand out. On the other hand, they are more difficult to put away in a wallet or business card holder, and a business card reader also can't read them. My advice is to use standard sizes and stand out in another way: logo, color, backside of the card...If you want to do something special with the card itself, try to have rounded corners (or one rounded corner)

- If it's applicable to your business, another way to stand out, is to use business cards with a **built-in magnet.** If you are in the home-delivery (like pizza) or plumber business, or another one that could benefit from being attached to the refrigerator. This is a great way of getting visibility.

- Another option is to use a CD-ROM as business card. This CD-ROM looks like a normal business card (same size and is printable), but is a bit thicker. On the CD-ROM you can put information about your company or free digital products. Before you pickup the telephone to order this kind of business card, I want to warn you that this is still an expensive alternative to paper. Another disadvantage is that only few people actually take the time to look at the information on CD-ROM, and almost everybody has Internet access nowadays, so they can look up this information on your website. If you want to stand out with your business card, a CD-ROM is still an original idea.

## How to deal with your own business cards?

- Make sure you have your business cards **always at hand:** in your wallet, at the office, in the car, at home...
- **Include your business card with all your letters and other communication material.** Contacts might throw away your marketing brochure, but are more likely to keep your business card.
- The same applies for all products, free samples...always include your business card.
- Use your business card as a **label on your briefcase** or suitcase. At receptions or other networking events, this helps other people to start a conversation.
- **Handle your business cards with care.** Don't give a card that is damaged. On a conscious and subconscious level people will start making negative associations with you as a person.
- **Use a business card holder with two pockets.** A business card holder is a small case the size of a standard business card. One pocket is for your own cards, the other pocket for the cards you receive. When you have the logo of your company or a nice picture printed on the business card holder, you also have another conversation starter.

## When to exchange business cards?

When do you best exchange business cards? When you meet? When you end the conversation or somewhere in the middle?

My advice is: "when appropriate." OK, this sounds like the answer of a sphinx, but I can't give you a better one. What I always do personally is first figure out what the other person is doing, what he is looking for at this moment or what his interests are. Then I think how I could help him with that: do I have information in this field? Do I know someone? If I can find a way I can be of service to him, I ask for his business card. This also solves the "problem of the follow up." Many people hunt for business cards, but don't know what to do with them afterwards. Then their "investment" in time, effort and sometimes money is largely wasted. Because I have been looking for ways to be of help and for commonalities from the beginning, I always have something to say or write about afterwards. This way I can start building a relationship with them.

Does this approach always work? No. I don't always find ways to be of service and I don't get along with everybody. In those cases there is a great chance that there is no exchange of business cards. Do I build a strong relationship with all people I did exchange business cards with? No, but at least our conversation was nice and I'm sure they will remember me (and I remember them) when we meet again. Maybe next time we will strengthen our relationship.

Some more tips about exchanging business cards:

- If you are at a networking event talking to a whole group of people, **try to avoid giving your business card at the same time as all the others.** Your card risks being "lost" in the mass of cards. Many people have difficulty remembering names. For many of them the business card is the link between a face and a name. Give your business card when you have one-on-one contact with a person. Take the time to read the business card, more or less "forcing" the other person to do the same. This way the link between your card and your face gets stronger.

- An exception to the previous tip is when you are in a group and get some time to introduce yourself to the whole group. Then you can give your card to the listeners.
- If you really can't get a one-on-one moment with a person, an alternative is to ask for her business card and **send your own business card by mail.** You also risk not having a link between your face and your business card, but you have the advantage to reach that person at a time more suited than at the busy event. Some well-known people get lots of business cards and if they can't remember who they got it from or why they got it, they just throw it away. When you send your card by mail, the chance that this happens is much smaller. You can also send an email, but this involves a risk, too. We all get so many emails each day, including SPAM, that an email from an unknown person might immediately be deleted.
- **In Asia business cards are presented and received with two hands.** This looks like a ritual of giving a present and that's exactly the reason why they do it this way. Contacts are very important to them, so they receive the necessary attention. What about you? How do you treat the business cards you receive? Do you want your business card (and yourself!) being treated as important? Then be an example and show interest in the business cards of others!
- **When you receive a business card from someone, don't put it away immediately.** In Asia, for example, this is an insult. You can learn a lot from a business card and find extra commonalities or things to talk about: function, department, location, logo, color of the card, and text on the back (or the reason why there is no text on the back)...

- **Ask for more than one business card.** Ask for a second one that you can pass on to someone else. The other person will be pleasantly surprised and will very likely remember you.

## How to deal with other people's business cards?

- Nowadays everybody works with a computer and with an email program. Most of these email programs are used as an address book. Some organizations have dedicated databases to store contact data. Whatever you use, I strongly recommend storing your contact data electronically. Make sure you make backups of these data yourself or have your IT department do this for you.
- If you don't have the time to put the data in yourself (although I strongly recommend doing this, as this will help you to remember names and faces), there are some alternatives:
  - Have a co-worker or secretary put the data in
  - Use a Business Card Reader to scan the business cards, recognize the text via OCR (Optical Character Recognition) and upload them in your software program. (See also tip about tools)
- Keep and store all the business cards you receive. You never know when you or someone from your network might need this person.

Why should you store the data electronically?

- **It's easier to find someone.** You can search in different fields or do a general search. A physical storage like a Rolodex or folder provides only one way to retrieve your contact. If you classify your business cards according to the name of the organization and you only remember the name of your contact person, then it will be hard to find the business card.

- A database or email program enables you to store **almost unlimited contacts** without taking much space. It is easy to take with you on a laptop or PDA and to transfer to other computers (like at work and home).
- Another reason for having the data in an electronic format is that there are **tools like Plaxo that help you to stay updated** when your contacts change function, department, organization...without you having to figure that out yourself. Read more about these tools in the next chapter about online networking.
- Note: despite all precautions sometimes things go wrong with electronics. That's why I advise you to **store the paper business cards as an emergency backup.** It's like insurance: you buy some hoping you'll never have to use it.

Don't see the above-mentioned tips as the only truth. You are always the best person to evaluate what to do in a given situation and to "break the rules" if that seems the best solution to you. By understanding the tips you will at least be more aware of what the consequences could be.

## Remembering names

Do you recognize the following story? At a reception of a network club: "Hi Dave, how are you? How is your business?" You have a vague recollection of this guy, but have no idea what his name is, so you say: "I'm fine, thank you. How are you?" and while the other guy is talking to you about his business, you are torturing your brain: "Who is this guy, who is this guy, why can't I remember his name?" You are so obsessed with remembering his name that you can't focus on his story and miss out on important information, and this is only the beginning of the evening. You know that lots of these encounters will follow.

A Belgian politician, Achiel Van Acker, had his own way of dealing with this. Instead of torturing his memory, he asked: "What was your name again?" When the other person told his last name, the politician replied: "I remembered that, but what was your first name again?" When he only got the first name, he just adapted his response: "Of course, I remember your first name, but what was your last name again?" Apparently, he got quite famous by doing this, but I rather go for the real stuff: really remembering names.

But how on earth do you do that?

Before I give you some tips, there is one very important issue: the biggest problem is not **remembering** people's names, but **storing** them in the first place!

If you're one of the people that use the excuse, (and yes, it's only an excuse!) "My parents both have bad memories, it runs in the family," you better think again. Everybody is equipped with a fantastic memory, but only a few know how to use it well.

## Two kinds of memories

The most important thing to know about memory is that you have two kinds of memory: a left brain memory and a right brain memory. They both have their specific characteristics. However, in Western society we are focused on the left brain, the part that is good at storing facts and numbers, but also the part of the memory that is much smaller than the right brain part.

The right brain memory works more visually. Not only pictures, but also smells, sounds, physical touch, taste and emotions. The more vividly the whole picture is stored, the more ways there are to retrieve it from your memory. The more action there is in the picture and the more exaggerated the picture is, the easier it will be to retrieve the image from the subconscious memory. Think of the subconscious memory as a five year old that exaggerates everything. If you know or knew kids of this age, remember their stories: "We were playing on a slide at least 30 feet high, we had to climb all the way up and we were sweating so hard, it was like taking a shower. When we came down the slide, we went faster than daddy's car. There was so much wind, like a giant hair dryer as big as our house…" Can you see and feel the picture? You can use this technique to your advantage. All you have to do is imagine this kind of picture and store it in your subconscious memory.

In short these are the things you have to keep in mind when using your subconscious memory:

- Use images (with all your senses, especially the sense that you developed best, for most people this means sight)
- Include action
- Exaggerate the scene
- Associate with other things

## Ten tips to remember names

You now know the basics to remembering things. Here are some extra tips that will help you remember names. They are based on the tips in Donna Fisher's book, "Personal Networking for Dummies."

1. **Make a priority of remembering names.** Train your memory. **Focus on recalling** names and after a while this will be much easier.
2. **First say that you can do it: remembering names.** Maybe the only reason why you can't do it is because you convinced yourself you can't or that it is something you inherited from your parents. This is not true. Everybody can train his memory and remember names.
3. **Concentrate** on making contact with people. Being distracted is the main reason why you don't store particular information. How do you feel when the person who you are talking to is constantly watching over your shoulder? You don't feel respected and your respect for the other person diminishes. If you know that you are easily distracted, position yourself so that you are facing a back wall instead of the entrance or the middle of the room.

4. **Listen attentively to what another person has to say. You can't remember or recall what you didn't hear.** Give the other person your full attention. This means: when the other person is speaking: don't think about what you are going to say yourself next or don't think about what you are going to do on the weekend. If you focus on your own thoughts, you won't hear what the other person tells you and you can't store it in your memory.

5. **Work with the name of the other person.** The process could look like this:

   a. You meet someone and he introduces himself. You **hear** the name. Ask again if you didn't understand it the first time.

   b. You **repeat** the name by integrating it in your reply: "Hi Frank, nice to meet you."

   c. You make a "picture" of the first and last name or make an association with the name of a person you already know (I use this association mostly for the first name, because it is not always easy to make a picture of a last name). You can make pictures or associations in different languages, with parts of the name, with the meaning of a name…or you can ask where the name comes from and remember that story.

   d. During the conversation you drop the name a **few times** in a **natural way** (if this doesn't come natural to you, you better skip this step, because it can work against you!): "Frank, tell me, how long have you been a member of this association?" I don't always recommend this step, because of two reasons:

      i. This is something sales people learn in a course and everybody knows that. When this happens, people get the feeling that you are applying the tricks of your sales course and raise their shield to hold off your sales pitch.

ii. When do you use the name of your partner or kids? Think about it for a second. Probably when you need them and you don't see them or when you are angry with them you call their name. So, using names is usually not part of natural conversation. I recommend that you only repeat the name of your contact in the conversation if it comes naturally to you.

e. If Frank is wearing a **nametag,** look at it, to **read** his name. (You can also begin with this step).

f. When you ask Frank for a **business card**, take the opportunity to **read** his name on the business card.

g. **Mention** the name at the **end of the conversation**: "Nice to have met you, Frank. Success with your business."

h. When you return **home or to the office**, you quickly look through the business cards you received and **think back** to every conversation. Make the associations of the name, his face, what you talked about, the environment, the name of the event, the organization ... Make as many associations as possible. See them before you and put action in your "pictures." This way they are stored the best.

i. **Type the information of the business cards in your email software or database. Make additional notes:** (it is also good networking behavior to do this directly after the conversation on the business card) to help you remember the person. Write down what you noticed about this person: a hobby or a particular topic you talked about.

Another tip concerning storing pictures and making associations: sometimes it's better not to tell the other person which association you made in your mind. If you associated John Hill with a toilet

("John" is slang for toilet) and Hill with the enormous wart on his nose, then you better keep this information to yourself.

6. Do your **follow up** as soon as possible. The faster the follow up, the faster the names are locked in a **permanent storage** in your own memory. An extra advantage is that **the other person will remember you better, too.**

7. Give meaning to the contact by **taking action.** Action reinforces content. This means: making an appointment, calling, sending an email... If you promised something during the conversation, really take action!

8. **Associate someone's name with something else.** Make a mental note, visualize something that helps you remember this person (e.g. a giant car for a car salesman).

9. **Use all your senses.** (see point 5). Be aware of how you recall things best. People are different. Think about your own situation.

    a. **Hearing:** listening to the name and pronouncing it yourself.

    b. **Sight:** looking at the name and really reading it.

    c. **Kinesthetic abilities:** writing down the name and typing it.

    d. Do this by:

        i. Looking **carefully** at people so you can create a good mental image.

        ii. Listening to the **sound of their voices** (rhythm, tone, accent, timbre...)

        iii. Being aware of the **feelings** you experience when you meet them or hear them talk.

        iv. **Making contact physically** by shaking hands when you meet someone and when you say goodbye.

10. Be aware of the most beautiful sound in the world. Dale Carnegie said that the sound of a person's own name is the most beautiful sound in the world. However, in my opinion this is not always communicated or trained in the right way in sales training courses (see point 5 d). What is the most beautiful thing is that next time you meet someone again you still remember his or her name. This shows you think this person is important enough to be remembered. Especially because so many people have trouble with remembering names, one of the ways to get noticed in a positive way is by calling people by their name the next time you meet them!

Stand out from the crowd by training your memory to remember names. This will be appreciated very much!

# Chapter 6

# Online networking and tools

When we speak about networking, most of us think of meeting people and going to events. As you already read in the previous chapters, networking is much more than that.

With the fast developments in communication technology there are also more opportunities, ways and mediums to communicate and, therefore, to network. There are lots of technology aids for networking. These include: email, instant messaging (like MSN Messenger and Yahoo Messenger), websites, blogs, forums, chat clubs, free telephone over the Internet (like Skype), add-ins for email software (like the toolbars of Plaxo and LinkedIn) and networking websites (like LinkedIn, Ecademy, Xing, Ryze and Spoke).

What is most important to remember is that we are talking about tools and aids when we consider online networking websites. They are a means, not a goal. They help you to network more efficiently and effectively. When people ask me: "What's best: online or offline networking?" my response is always: "The combination of both." Online networking helps your offline networking efforts and vice versa.

In this chapter you will get some examples of these networking aids and how to use them. I will focus on tools that are available for free or almost free. I could also recommend expensive software, but that would be an extra barrier to start or improve your networking actions, and that's something I want to avoid.

Networking is part of your day-to-day life and should as, a consequence, have a reasonable price, with regard to money and time.

## Email software and add-ins

Probably the most widespread communication medium today is email. The most commonly used email software is MS Outlook. That's why most suppliers of other communication tools provide links and add-ins for this software. I will limit this section about email to MS Outlook because this is not only the most common software for email, but for most people it comes standard with their professional or personal computer. You don't have to make an extra investment. If you work with other software, take some time to look at how these tips can be applied to your situation. Even better: ask an email expert from your network to help you out on this.

In this section you will first see how you can use MS Outlook to network more efficiently. Then you will be presented some add-ins (like toolbars or menus) that can give your efficiency an extra boost.

### Tips to get MS Outlook help you to network more efficiently

Most people know how to send and receive an email and use the "Contacts" of MS Outlook to store data about the people they know. However, there are some features that few people know, but that could help you increase your networking efficiency.

#### *Signature*

A "signature" is the part at the bottom of the email with your contact data. It is very helpful for the receiver of your email to have this information. Especially if it's the first contact the two of you have. Another reason for including your signature is that many people are not organized very well. They don't store the contact data in the "Contact" section of MS Outlook. If they want to contact you they will search for your email.

***Networking success tip: Help others to help you: use a signature in your emails.***

In order to avoid having to write your signature over and over again and make errors, you could use the signature function of MS Outlook. In MS Outlook 2002 you will find the signature at this location: Tools/Options/Mailformat and then at the bottom "Signature."

You can make different signatures. This can be useful if you have two jobs, or if you have a (official) function in an association or want a separate signature for your personal email. But don't forget to change the default signature when sending out an email!

In MS Outlook 2002 you toggle between your signatures at this location: Insert/Signature (this menu is available when you are actually writing an email).

### *Contacts*

I strongly recommend storing the contact data of the people from your network in the "Contacts" section of MS Outlook. Not only to retrieve information faster yourself, but also to be able to pass these data on to others. If you have them right at hand, it will be no trouble for you to pass this data on. If you need half an hour to retrieve them, you will be less motivated to do this. Don't create barriers for your networking actions. Store the contact data in your "Contacts."

***Networking success tip: don't create barriers for connecting people: store your contact data in your e-mail software.***

Some tips about storing contact data:

- **Fill in at least the name, company, (mobile) telephone number and email address.**

- **Use "categories"** (when you open a "contact" you will see it at the bottom on the right). Personally, I use "categories" for: type of contact (customer, supplier, partner, personal...) and where we first met (name of the event). This helps me to remember them better, group them and retrieve them faster if I don't remember their name or company anymore. Using "categories" also helps to filter and group people.
- **Use the "notes" section** (the large white space). Write down keywords that help you remember this person. Copy the things you wrote on the backside of the business card and add some extra information. Write down what you talked about, common interests and contacts, things that struck you, the person that introduced you to each other... In short, note down everything that helps you to remember this person and keep in touch afterwards.
- Fill in the other "fields" if you have the data and if you have the time to do this.

Some people think filling in the contact data of the people they met is a waste of time. Personally, I don't agree with that because it forces you to think about this person again. This way he will be stored better in your memory.

If you don't want to fill in the data, there is another aid for you: a **business card reader.** This is a small scanner that comes with OCR (Optical Character Recognition) software. This is how it works:

- You scan the business card
- You run the OCR process
- You check if the data is recognized correctly. (Although the software works pretty well, not all data is recognized 100%, especially when a company name is embedded in a fancy graphic logo)
- You upload them in your email software, customer relationship database or in a spreadsheet

Some examples of business card readers are:

- Iris Business Card Reader: www.irislink.com
- Cardscan: www.cardscan.com
- Bizcardreader: www.bizcardreader.com

Let's assume you have scanned the contacts or filled in the data by hand. Now you have the data about your network contacts available in your "Contacts." You can start using them.

I don't know about you, but for me the standard overview of my "Contacts" in MS Outlook confuses me rather than helps me. Some "contact cards" are bigger than others because I have more information about those people. It is also impossible to sort or filter the fields. But there is a solution.

By default MS Outlook offers some other views that you can use. This could help you. Only a few people know this, but within a minute you can have another view of the data, completely the way you want it. Personally, I prefer a spreadsheet-like list with rows and columns, and only with a few fields: name, organization, telephone number, categories and email.

In MS Outlook 2002 you can change the overview of your contacts on this location: View/Current View/Define Views

You will find more tips about contacts in a next section about the add-ins from Plaxo and LinkedIn:

- How to keep your contact data up-to-date
- How to get the contact data out of an email and into a "contact card" with only two clicks of the mouse
- How to automatically make new contact cards for all (or some) email addresses out of email messages, in whatever folder they are stored

## *Your own VCard*

"What's a Vcard?" you might ask. A VCard is more or less your electronic business card. The "contact card" of MS Outlook is such a VCard.

Make in your email software a "contact card" or Vcard for yourself. Why? You can send it as attachment to people via email. This way they don't have to put all the data in themselves from your business card or from your email signature. You make it easier for them to connect with you. This is a very good follow up action.

You can also use the notes section to provide extra data about yourself. This could be about yourself or what you have to offer. Some people write down their 50 words. If you need some inspiration, you can look at your networking profile and the part of the Golden Triangle about giving.

## *Rules wizard*

If you are like me and you have many contacts and many subscriptions to eZines, you can be overwhelmed by an email avalanche. Some help to manage emails is welcome in such situations. One of the tools that can help you is the "rules wizard" of MS Outlook.

This tool helps you to create "rules" to handle your emails automatically. For example, you can make a "rule" to automatically put the monthly eZine "ABC News" in the folder "eZine ABC News," or you can automatically forward the messages from a specific project to the project team members.

There are 2 ways of doing this in MS Outlook 2002:

- Via Tools/Rules Wizard
- Click with the right mouse button on an email and then choose "Create rule"

## *Email templates*

If you meet lots of people at events and you want to connect with them afterwards via email, this can be very time consuming. At one of my first networking events I connected with 12 people. I wanted to do a good follow up and write them all a personalized email. Personalized because I wanted these people to remember me. So, I wrote about the event where we met (I gave the context), showed that I really listened (I gave some details from the conversation), gave the information I promised (websites, articles...) and provided some information about my own business. It took me about 10 minutes per email. In total this came down to two hours. Only to reconnect! I felt that this was a major obstacle for me to keep following up, so I examined how MS Outlook could help me. That's how I discovered the email templates called "forms." In fact, making an email template (or "form") is rather simple.

- You write an email and save it as "Outlook template" (with *.oft extension). *Caution: you don't have this option when you use MS Word as editor.*
- If you want to use this template you can find it in MS Outlook 2002 at this location: Tools/Form/Choose Form, then choose in the "Look in" drop down box at the top: "User templates in file system" and finally pick the template you want.

Please use these templates in an intelligent way! Always personalize them. Use a template as a basis to start from. For example, you can make a template for the event that you attended last night. You already filled in the context and the information you want to provide about yourself. For every person you then start from this template to add details about your conversation and the information you promised to provide. For me the use of templates reduced the time needed to reconnect via email by 75%.

You can also include attachments in your email templates. A good idea is to include your VCard.

## *Reminders for birthdays*

A great time to reconnect with someone is when it's her birthday. In general, this applies to your personal circle and your co-workers, but in some cases you can also send a birthday card to a customer, supplier or business partner.

The only problem is remembering a person's birthday. Most people use birthday calendars, but forget to look at them, or notice the birthday when it's already two weeks later.

Do you recognize this? Then you can use MS Outlook to help you. The only thing you have to do is put in the birthday in this person's contact card (you find it in the second "tab," called "details"). When it's the big day, MS Outlook automatically reminds you.

Then you can take action: have lunch/dinner, have a present or flowers delivered, send a card by mail, send an eCard or email. Remember: the more effort you put in, the better the response. Nowadays it is very easy to send an email. If you send a hand written birthday card (that you had to go out to buy) your contact will appreciate this much more!

The most important part is to reconnect, and if for the moment the only thing you can do is to send an email, do that. It's better than doing nothing.

## Plaxo toolbar for MS Outlook (and Outlook Express)

Do you know that every year 10% of the population moves or changes work? This could mean that all your contact data is worthless in 10 years. How can you be sure to have the latest information from people? Some of them will tell you, send a card with a new address or provide you with the new contact data via email, but what about all the others, especially people you don't meet very often? One of the tools that can help you solve this problem is Plaxo. There are other tools that are similar, but most people use Plaxo at this moment.

## *What is Plaxo?*

If you haven't heard of it yet, chances are that you nevertheless came in contact with it. With Plaxo people can send emails to verify if contact data of their contacts is still accurate.

Plaxo consists of two things: the website www.plaxo.com and a toolbar for MS Outlook and Outlook Express that can be downloaded for free from this website. The website itself is useful if you don't have MS Outlook or Outlook Express or in situations where you don't have access to your own computer. Personally, I never use the website, but only the toolbar in MS Outlook.

## *How can Plaxo help you?*

- The contact data of other people who use Plaxo is constantly up-to-date. You don't have to do anything yourself. If they change their contact data, these modifications are automatically carried through in MS Outlook on your computer.
- You can send people requests to check and update their contact data. You can send one message to all your contacts, but please, at least personalize your message. Don't use the default message of Plaxo. People (maybe including yourself) are really turned off by this kind of impersonal email.
- When you use the feature "build your address book" Plaxo searches for email addresses in the emails stored in the folders in MS Outlook you choose. They are checked with your existing contacts. If you want, you can make a "contact card" for the found email addresses. Combined with the feature of requesting people to see if their contact data are still up-to-date, this is a very powerful and easy way to always keep your address book up-to-date.

- You keep your contacts up-to-date of changes in your life. When you change the data in your "Plaxo cards" all people who also use Plaxo automatically get an email that notifies them of the changes. These changes are also carried through in their "Contacts" folder.
- With Plaxo you can also create a signature for your emails. This has more graphical options than the standard signature from MS Outlook. What is nice to know, is that Plaxo has a partnership with www.iprint.com. They print your Plaxo business card on paper for a low price.
- People can also fill in their birthdays on their Plaxo cards. Plaxo automatically notifies you a week before with an email. They were smart enough to team up with websites that offer eCards, paper birthday cards (www.artamata. com), flowers (www.growerflowers.com), gifts (www.redenvelope.com) and books (www.barnesandnoble.com). If you tend to forget birthdays and birthday presents, this service might be something for you.

  This is also a nice example of commercial networking. Plaxo teams up with other parties that their users might benefit from. What about your organization? Who can you team up with? Even if you're not in a commercial role, think about how collaborating with other departments or other teams might benefit the both of you and your (internal) customers.

How could Plaxo be useful within larger companies? If you change function or department and modify your Plaxo card, all connected persons will be notified. This will give them an opportunity to contact you again. Use this opportunity to reconnect yourself when you see that there are changes in the function, company or department of someone you are connected to.

## *How to avoid filling in your contact data over and over again*

If you don't have MS Outlook or if your organization doesn't allow you to install the toolbar in MS Outlook, you can still use the website. This avoids having to fill in over and over again the requests other people send. If your data is on the server of Plaxo, other people automatically receive this information when requesting an update from you, so you're never bothered again. Make sure that you update your contact data when you move or change work.

### *Is Plaxo safe?*

Some people are afraid to use tools like Plaxo. They fear they are going to be SPAMMED with ads for Viagra, online gambling and other similar stuff. My own experience and a small survey with people from my network tell me that this is not the case with Plaxo. Of course, you never know what's going to happen in the future, but for the moment it seems to be safe.

In short: I strongly recommend using Plaxo (or a similar tool). It really helps a lot in staying in touch with your network.

## LinkedIn Outlook toolbar

Wouldn't it be nice if you didn't have to cut and paste the contact data from an email by hand, but let the computer do this for you?

Then you definitely have to download the free Outlook toolbar from LinkedIn (www.linkedin.com) LinkedIn is one of the websites that are dedicated to online networking. More about the website in a next section. Let's focus on the toolbar.

Despite the high value of this toolbar, it is not easy to find on the website and they tend to move it to other pages. At the time of writing you can find this toolbar via the menu "Tools" at the bottom of the page. Don't confuse this "LinkedIn Outlook" toolbar with the "Linked IE toolbar" that is featured on the top on the right on the homepage.

These are the functions of this "LinkedIn Outlook" toolbar:

- **Grab:** when you receive an email from one of your contacts that is not yet in your "Contacts," you simply select his signature and push the "Grab" button. Automatically a "contact card" is created with the data you selected in the right fields. Similar to a business card reader this function doesn't always work 100% of the time, and you have to check if the data is in the correct fields, but it is a tremendous time saver!

- **Collect:** this works the same way as the "build address book" function of Plaxo.
- **Invite:** make a template for inviting people to connect with you on the LinkedIn website and send the email.
- **Upload:** you can upload some or all of your contacts from Outlook to the LinkedIn website. Automatically the website checks which of your contacts already use LinkedIn. Obviously, they are the first to connect with.

You can use the "Grab" function to avoid typing all contact data by hand. If you use the LinkedIn website to connect with other people, I strongly recommend using the other functionalities, too.

## Stay up-to-date easily with your contacts using Plaxo, LinkedIn and Xing

You know now that Plaxo and LinkedIn exist. You also know that Plaxo is an add-in to keep your contacts up-to-date, and that the LinkedIn toolbar has a handy "grab" functionality plus a feature to upload your contacts to the LinkedIn website.

How can you use these tools to help you to stay up-to-date with your contacts without spending too much time?

This is a strategy you can use:

1. **Retrieve email addresses from emails**
   - Use in MS Outlook the Plaxo "build your address book" or LinkedIn "collect" option to search all the folders of MS Outlook for email addresses that are not yet in your "Contacts."

- Select the email addresses you want a "contact card" for (for example, you don't want a contact card for general and impersonal email addresses like info@company_abc.com).

**2. Get updated information via Plaxo**

- Wait a few hours after the previous actions. Plaxo will automatically check if the email addresses belong to a Plaxo member. If this is the case, the "contact card" of this person on your PC is automatically updated with all the information this person provided in his Plaxo card.

**3. Get updated information via LinkedIn and Xing**

- In MS Outlook use the "upload" function of LinkedIn. On the website of LinkedIn all the members get a small icon. Connect with them – they will be more than happy to connect with you! Xing offers a similar toolbar for MS Outlook. All the other networking websites will probably follow soon with similar functionality.
- On the website of LinkedIn look at the people that accepted your connection and download their VCard if they are not a Plaxo member.
- Now you have the latest data from a lot of people and have expanded your network at LinkedIn.

**4. Get updated information from people who don't use Plaxo, LinkedIn or Xing yet**

- Use the Plaxo "update contacts" tool. First select the people you want to send an email to with the request to review their data. Then personalize the email (don't use the standard invitation please!).
- Use the LinkedIn "invite" tool in MS Outlook to select the contacts you want to be connected to via LinkedIn, or upload your contacts to the LinkedIn website and invite them via the website. You can do the same for your Xing contacts.

I advise you to repeat this process at least every six months, especially Step 1. Depending on the results of this step you might choose to do the other steps as well.

## Instant Messaging

One of the tools that probably out performs email as the most used communication medium is instant messaging.

Instant messaging comes down to exchanging text messages via the Internet in real time. You need an application to do this. The difference with email is that these messages are "in real time" and are used for instant dialogue as an alternative for speaking on the phone.

What many people don't know is that most instant messaging tools offer the possibility to have group conversations. This can be very useful if you have to solve a problem together with people that are in different parts of the world.

The most popular free instant messaging tools are:

- MSN Messenger: www.msnmessenger.com
- Yahoo Messenger: messenger.yahoo.com
- AOL Instant Messenger: www.aim.com
- ICQ: www.icq.com (abbreviation for "I seek you")
- Jabber: www.jabber.org

Young people mostly use these instant-messaging tools to communicate with their friends, but more and more organizations are adopting them as an extra communication tool, especially for communication with colleagues or partners in other locations, being on another floor of the same building or in a country on the other side of the globe.

## Free telephone over the Internet: Skype

When you want to stay in touch with people over the phone, this can be rather expensive. An alternative is free telephone over the Internet via Skype.

Not only can you call people one-on-one all over the world, but you can also have group conversations. Skype also has instant messaging options: while speaking you can also exchange written messages with another person which is very handy when you have a difficult name of a website you want the other person to look at.

Don't be scared by this new technology. It's easy to use and free. You only have to download the free software from www.skype.com. The only small purchase you will want to make is a headset. You can do without one, but you risk having a lower quality conversation.

Note: Skype is not completely 100% free: it won't work properly without broadband service. If you already pay for broadband, you won't have extra costs for PC-to-PC communication. Skype also allows calling to (mobile) telephones, but then you have to pay a small fee. This service is called Skype Out. Another way (Skype In) is offered: you can rent a regular telephone number (voice mail included). The call is routed to Skype wherever you are in the world. Skype In and Out still cost money, but it is far cheaper than calling via (mobile) telephone.

## Online networking websites

A great way of connecting with people locally and globally is via online networks. These are websites that are set up to give people a platform to connect and network with each other. In September 2003 there was a real breakthrough and they are now used by millions of people worldwide, and they are here to stay.

Andrew Forbes from www.earlystage.com makes a comparison between the use of letters as a business interaction tool and online networking as part of business networking. In 1984, all business communication was done via letters. We didn't use email or instant messaging because it didn't exist yet (or was only available for the happy few). In 2004, the amount of letters decreased in favor of email and instant messaging. What's more important is that the total transaction value of communication and especially volume increased a lot. The downside is that the quality of the average communication has decreased. You can see the same happening with "in person" networking. Within 10 years this will be only a small part of all "networking actions." Online networking actions will outnumber "in person" networking by far.

If you look at the advantages of online networking this is no surprise:

- Regardless of **Time**: you (or at least your profile) are present 24 hours a day, 7 days a week, 365 days a year. You check your messages when you choose to, be it 11 o'clock in the morning or in the middle of the night.
- Regardless of **Place**: you can access these online networks from anywhere in the world, as long as you have an Internet connection. You can do it from your own home, in your pajamas if you like.
- Both **Local and Global**: you can connect with people from your own town or country, or even with people from another part of the world.
- **Targeted**: you can use keywords, (company) names or other relevant data to find the right people for you and your network. Most networking websites have excellent search functionalities.
- **Passive presence.** While you are sleeping, people will find you (your profile). Be sure to make a good profile, so people (and search engines) can find you.
- **Memory-proof**: if you don't remember what a person looks like or forgot about the details of her business, you can look up her profile.
- **Easy group forming**: you can start or join a club or forum of people with interest in the same subject. In the "real" world it is sometimes very difficult to arrange physical meetings with these people (supposing that you were able to find them in the first place).

- **Efficient**: you can connect online with far more people than you could ever meet face to face on a daily basis.
- **Reduced time and expense**: you don't have to travel, order drinks or food and sacrifice your work or family time.
- **High visibility**: Online networking websites get lots of visitors and links from other websites. As a consequence, your profile appears high in search engines like Google. If you don't like this feature, some websites (like Ecademy) offer the possibility to hide your profile from being indexed by search engines.

The only potential dangers for online networking are the lack of knowledge about how to interact with other people via these networking websites. I will share more about that in the section about online etiquette.

## Different types of online networks

Online networks are a relatively new medium, but a very strong one, with their own characteristics. There are several websites that are (partly) dedicated to networking. Some of them focus on the more social aspect of friends and family (and are more related to dating sites). Others are more dedicated to business networking. Depending on the type of website you get more features and ways of communicating.

Hendrik Deckers (www.hendrikdeckers.com) made an overview of these networks in 2004. Although things change rapidly and especially on the Internet, this is the best overview I found yet.

In short he makes a distinction between:

- **Social BUSINESS communities**. The focus is on business. Websites that belong to this category are: www.ecademy.com, www.Xing.com, www.ryze.com,www.spoke.com

- **SOCIAL business communities**. The emphasis is on the social aspect. Examples: www.orkut.com, www.tribe.net, www.craigslist.org
- **Business network platforms**. These websites don't focus on the community aspect, but can be seen more as platforms to connect. The best known among them is www.linkedin.com.
- **Relationship management tools**. Under this category fall websites that offer tools or solutions to connect people or to make connections between people visible. Examples: www.plaxo.com, www.tacit.com, www.visiblepath.com

There are lots of online networks. You can't join them all. To help you to make a decision on where to start, these are the online networks I recommend at the time of writing this book:

| Name | URL | Reason for recommendation |
|---|---|---|
| Ecademy | www.ecademy.com | • Very helpful community, with a focus on the human aspect.<br>• Motto: "People first, business second"<br>• Global and local<br>• Online combined with offline: local meetings to meet other members in person, which strengthens the relationships |
| LinkedIn | www.linkedin.com | • Very large user base<br>• Highly accepted in small and large companies<br>• Based on the 6 degrees of proximity concept: you can see who your own contacts are linked to<br>• Remark: this is not a community, but more like the yellow pages |

| Name | URL | Reason for recommendation |
|---|---|---|
| Xing | www.Xing.com | • Multilingual user interface<br>• Large user base (especially in Europe)<br>• Online combined with offline: local meetings to meet other members in person, which strengthens the relationships |
| Ryze | www.ryze.com | • Large user base (especially in USA)<br>• Online combined with offline: local meetings to meet other members in person, which strengthens the relationships |

A more elaborate list of online networks can be found at the Social Software weblog: http://socialsoftware.weblogsinc.com/sns-meta-list

If you want to read more about the differences between the networks, you can read the whole presentation in the profile of Hendrik Deckers at Ecademy.

Another great source for an overview of online networks is www.thevirtualhandshake.com the website of Scott Allen and David Teten. Also read their book, "The Virtual Handshake," if you want to go deeper into the subject of online networking.

## What can you expect from online networks?

There are some people who think online networks are the (next) Holy Grail, and focus all their efforts on this, while neglecting other parts of their business and personal life.

Although online networking requires some effort in the beginning to learn about the several functionalities of the specific online network you're using, it is worth your time. I recommend doing it at your own pace otherwise, you might get frustrated. Keep in mind that this is another way of networking. These online networks are just another medium to do the same: getting in touch with people, help them and be helped.

Too many sales people think online networking is the ultimate way to boost their sales, and in the end it is, but in the same way as networking at events and with your own network on the phone, via email and in person. Don't expect that online networks will satisfy all your short term needs!

If you network on these online networks with the "Give and Receive" attitude, you will get some (significant) results. Geert Conard, one of the members on Ecademy, told me that 90% of his business came via online networks. He also wrote a book about his experiences with online networks: "A Girlfriend in Every City." You can find more testimonials about the results of online networking on Ecademy via this link: www.ecademy.com/node.php?id=4155

I want to emphasize again that networking and also online networking is not for sales people alone. If you are looking for a new employee, business partner, supplier, source of information or a new job, online networks will help you a lot!

## Some online networking tips

Since online networking is rather new, many people don't know what the best strategy is to deal with it. Online networking guru, Scott Allen has 10 online networking tips. I give some additional information so they become clearer to you.

1. **Remember, you're connecting with people.** Although you use technology, normal communication rules and behavior still apply. Read the next section about online networking etiquette.

2. **Clarify what you have to give and what you want to gain.** Be clear about what you have to offer, especially besides the products and services of the company you work for. Don't sell. Be sure to mention what you are looking for. This way you not only get what you want more rapidly, but you also give people the opportunity to help you. Remember: don't ask for sales, this turns people off.

3. **Become an information center.** Gather knowledge and distribute it. Get to know people and connect them to each other.
4. **Be personally visible on the Internet.** Make a profile and include a picture. Use a recent picture so people can recognize you when you meet them at an event.
5. **Pick online communities that work for you.** There are too many online networks to join them all. Pick the one(s) that suit you best. You can start with the online networks I recommended in the previous section.
6. **Review the online community as a guest before you join.** Try a few and stick with the ones you are most comfortable with. Ask existing members about their experiences.
7. **Be prepared.** Have a profile; know what you have to offer and what you are looking for. Be willing to contribute to the clubs and forums, share your knowledge and connect with people.
8. **Pace yourself.** Have a life outside the online networks. In the end (online) networking should help you win time, not waste it more.
9. **Manage your email.** Respond to requests, but not at the cost of your own time (see also the tips about "Getting requests: the power of saying "no" on page 79).
10. **Be sensitive to people's time and email boxes.** Don't SPAM people with requests. Give them time to answer. If you really need a quick response, use the phone (see also the tips about "When to use which communication medium?" on page 234)

## Your online profile

It's very important to have a good online profile. This is your representation on the network platform you choose, 24 hours a day, 7 days a week and 365 days a year.

Part of your success (whatever that may be for you) depends on this profile. The other part depends on your interactions and contributions, but this takes time. Filling in your profile is only a small one-time investment. Of course, you have to update your profile, but the amount of time you spend on that is negligible.

In the chapter about "Your networking profile" (on page 103) you find an elaborate manual about the ingredients of your networking profile. Use them to create your own online profile. Keep one thing in mind: don't turn your profile into a sales pitch. Don't forget to include the personal stuff. That's what people relate to. That's the best way to find common ground.

It is a good idea to look at examples of people who are already members of the online network you choose.

## Online networking etiquette

As I already mentioned online networking is just another way of networking. The rules of normal human behavior still apply. Unfortunately, not everybody is aware of this, and that's understandable, because it's new. I'd like you to read the following "conversation" I had with one of the people on LinkedIn. This is the word-by-word translation of our correspondence:

- Original message of this contact that he wanted me to forward to somebody else I'm linked with: "Hi xxx, can we arrange an appointment?"
- I replied: "I will gladly forward your message and connect you to my contact, but could you give some more information regarding why you want to get in touch with him?"
- His reply: "Because we might have a good solution for them."
- I replied: "I'm sure you do, but can you be more specific? I get several requests a day and I don't want to SPAM my network with pointless messages. I would be glad if they did the same for me. If you could tell me why

I should connect you to him, then I can give you kind of an endorsement as well. This might increase your chances of doing business with him."

- That was the last message. I never heard from him after that. I'm sure this guy isn't so bad at all, but he opportunistically used the system of LinkedIn to get appointments for his sales calls. I would have gladly given him the opportunity to do so, if he showed me that he wanted to put some effort in it, too. In normal conversations, you don't do this either, do you?

You can imagine that since this "conversation" I am even more cautious about with whom to link. This kind of message could ruin your own reputation with your network, not only by writing them, but also by forwarding them.

Be a connector, but also a gatekeeper. Your network will be glad if you only forward messages that have "value," and your relationship will be strengthened. After a while opportunities will come your way, too.

These are my online networking etiquette tips:

- Golden rule: this is still about human communication. Communicate like you are talking to someone in person. All the rules of normal networking apply. Especially don't try to sell at once or go for your own win only!
- Many online networking websites and tools offer standard messages. Don't use them! Write your own message, or at least personalize the standard message!
- If you write a message:
    - State why you are contacting the other person and not somebody else, show your appreciation
    - Share your goal or show what's in it for them
    - Mention the things you have in common: interests and/or contacts
    - Build a relationship, don't sell yourself or ask too much in the first contact

- If you write a request:
  - Give context, without writing several pages
  - Keep all involved people up-to-date about the result of your request
- If you get a request to forward a message:
  - Be a connector and a gatekeeper
  - Endorse people whenever you can
  - Follow up with both parties
- If you have a "conversation" with someone like I did in the example
  - Always assume that the other person has good intentions
  - Don't write anything you wouldn't say in person either

Marc Freedman, the Director of the Dallas Blue Network, gathered messages that you can use to "educate" your network. For example: a message to decline a request or to decline an endorsement. Together with some other excellent links, you can find them under the "Stationary" menu at his website: www.dallasblue.com/linkedin.htm

## What do online networks have to offer?

Although there is a danger that at the time that you read this, the functionality of these networks has changed, I want to give you some ideas what online networks have to offer and how to use them.

## What do social business networks have to offer?

Examples of social business networks are Ecademy, Xing and Ryze.

In this table you will find the different functionalities these websites offer, how they may benefit you, and some extra tips.

| Feature | Benefits and tips |
|---|---|
| Online profile | • You have a representation 24/24, 7/7 and 365/365.<br>• You can read other people's profiles and learn about their interests, needs and wants. This increases the odds to connect. |
| Search | • Simple and advanced search functionalities allow you to find the people you're looking for.<br>• The more accurate other people will find information you provide about yourself, the higher the chance you will be found by other people. |
| Clubs or forums | • You can connect with other people with the same interest. Topics could be professional or personal.<br>• Be sure to join one or more clubs.<br>• You can start your own club, increasing your profile and perceived expertise |
| Blogs | • Some online networks offer blogs (your own space to write) within their own website. This is an alternative way of communicating with the other members, independently from the forums.<br>• These blogs are also accessible for search engines, leveraging your writing effort.<br>• Read the blogs of others and comment on them if you have a valuable contribution to make. This helps to get more visibility, show your experience to others and build trust.<br>• More on blogs in a next section. |
| Your network's network | • This functionality differs from website to website. After a search for a person you can almost always see the contacts you have in common. Then you can ask these common contacts to connect you to the person you're looking for. |
| Profile hits | • You can see which people visited your profile. This gives you the opportunity to contact them and get in touch. |

| Feature | Benefits and tips |
|---|---|
| In- and out-boxes | • You can communicate via the messaging system of the websites. This way your email address remains hidden in the first contact. Afterwards you can choose to communicate via the website or via regular email. |
| Testimonials | • People can leave a testimonial for you and endorse you. This helps to build trust with other contacts.<br>• Write testimonials for other people. They will appreciate this and maybe write one for you, too. But only write things that are true and without expecting to get something back. |
| Offline events | • You can connect with other people in person. This strengthens the relationship you built via the online platform.<br>• Most websites allow you to see who will be attending and print this list (on Ecademy even with a picture). This allows you to prepare yourself optimally. |

Please note that some of these functionalities are not available in the free memberships of these networking platforms. However, most memberships are not that expensive. Before you decide to join, you can always consider a trial membership first.

### *What do business network platforms have to offer?*

The best-known example of a business network platform is LinkedIn. LinkedIn is not a community, but more of a directory of people. It lacks the communication functionalities from the social business networks, but has other advantages. The first advantage is that the barrier to become a member is lower. It comes as no surprise that LinkedIn has more members than the social business networks. There are also more passive members.

In this table you will find the different functionalities LinkedIn offers and how they may benefit you.

| Feature | Benefits and tips |
|---|---|
| Online profile | • You have a representation 24/24, 7/7 and 365/365.<br>• You can read other people's profiles and learn about their interests, needs and wants. This gives you a higher chance to connect. |
| Search | • Simple and advanced search functionalities allow you to find the people you're looking for.<br>• The more accurate information you provide about yourself the higher chance you will be found by other people. |
| Groups | • Because there are no forums, this is only a gathering of people, communicating with each other via other platforms. Examples are alumni from universities or professional associations.<br>• Join or start your own alumni group and (re) connect with people from the university or college where you studied. The bonds between those people can be very powerful! |
| Your network's network | • One of the most powerful features of LinkedIn. After a search on somebody LinkedIn tells you via how many degrees (people) you can reach this person.<br>• Use the power of your network's network to connect with the people you are looking for. You can use the messaging system of LinkedIn (where you can follow the progress) or use the phone to get an introduction. |
| Jobs | • Next to connecting people with each other, LinkedIn is increasingly becoming a tool to find a new job or to find a new co-worker.<br>• Job offers can be posted here. It's not free, but way cheaper than other channels. This way it is becoming a threat to the more classic job websites and papers and other recruitment channels.<br>• If you are looking for a job or looking to hire someone, give this website a try! |

| Feature | Benefits and tips |
|---|---|
| Testimonials | • People can leave a testimonial for you and endorse you. This helps to build trust with other contacts.<br>• Write testimonials for other people. They will appreciate this and maybe write one for you too, but only write things that are true and without expecting to get something back. |
| Toolbars | • LinkedIn offers many toolbars for other programs (MS Outlook, Internet Explorer, Firefox) to combine the power of your email software or Internet browser with the features of LinkedIn. (See also the previous section about the LinkedIn Outlook toolbar) |

## How to use Google to support you in your networking actions?

Google can be a great ally in your networking efforts. Few people know all the features this website offers, so let's first start with the basics.

Have you ever been told "I Googled you yesterday?" As you might guess, this means that he typed your name in Google to see what is written about you on the web.

Have you already Googled yourself? No? Do it. You might be surprised!

Be sure to "Google" other people. People who are already in your network or people who you have an appointment with for the first time. Google might provide you with excellent background information.

Everybody knows Google from its search engine, but there are more free tools that can help you in your networking efforts:

- Google Toolbar: for your web browser. No need to go to the website of Google anymore. Just put in your search in the box in the toolbar.

- Google Desktop Search: you can't find a document or file about one of your networking contacts anymore on your PC? Then this tool can help you out.
- Google Print: search the full text of books (print.google.com)
- Google Scholar: search in scholarly papers (scholar.google.com)
- Search features: several aids to search the Web faster and get better and more personalized results (www.google.com/help/features.html)

You can find an overview of these extra tools on: www.google.com/options.

There are many other tools like maps, satellite pictures, translation tools, currency converters, calculators, weather forecasts and photograph editors available. Google keeps inventing and testing them in their lab (labs.google.com/). So, visit these pages on a regular basis to find out how your online (networking) ventures can be made easier.

A company called Soople has conveniently gathered lots of these options on one page at (www.soople.com). You can even create your own personalized version of this "dashboard!"

One of the alternatives for Google as a search engine is Dogpile (www.dogpile.com) This is a meta search engine, meaning that it is not a search engine itself, but that it groups several search engines like Google, MSN, Yahoo and Ask Jeeves.

Use these tools to help you prepare your online networking efforts and your attendance at networking events!

## Blogs: what are they and what do they have to do with networking?

Something completely different to the features of Google are blogs. But what is a blog?

The word "blog" is an abbreviation of "weblog." Mostly it is defined as an online journal that is published frequently (often daily). Readers can post comments on each journal entry. A blog has the appearance of a website. The main difference between a blog and a normal website is that a blog is more about opinions while most websites are places to give information or promote products.

Some examples of blogs with regard to networking are:

- **The Virtual Handshake** (by Scott Allen and David Teten) about online networking: www.thevirtualhandshake.com
- **Never Eat Alone** (by Keith Ferrazzi) about his opinion on networking and how he does it: nevereatalone.typepad.com
- **The Networking Coach's Opinion** (my blog) about networking in general: www.janvermeiren.com

One of the reasons I write about blogging in this book is that blogging is booming. According to the blogwatchers of Technorati (www.technorati.com) in August 2005 a new blog was started every second. In March 2005 there were 7.8 million blogs. This almost doubled to 14.7 million in August 2005, only five months later! Also, the fact that Microsoft launched MSN Spaces (www.msnspaces.com) with free blog functionality means that blogging becomes mainstream.

What do blogs have to do with networking?

It comes down to showing your expertise and linking with the readers of your blog and with other bloggers. This way you build trust. A nice side effect is that search engines like blogs and prefer them to "commercial" websites. Why? Blogs are supposed to have more content and less publicity. Company websites are often viewed as a marketing tool and, as a consequence, are considered less reliable with regard to objective content.

"Is blogging something for me?" you might ask. Yes it is. It is for everybody – all types of people blog. Many people use a blog as an online diary for their friends and family.

Others use it in a professional way: industry experts, CEO's of small and large companies, journalists and employees. So, it is also for you.

The main advantage of blogs is that they are freely available and have an easy and fast set up. In less than 10 minutes you should be able to create your own blog, without having to know anything about creating and maintaining websites. Give it a try yourself!

If you want to start your own blog, you could consider the following free services:

- Blogger: www.blogger.com
- Wordpress: www.wordpress.com
- MSN Spaces: www.msnspaces.com
- Blog.com: www.blog.com
- Abilon: www.abilon.org

You can find a short video to show you how easy it is (and fast!) to get your own blog at: www.businessownerscoachingclub.com/videos/Blogger-firstblog.html

If you want more functionality for your blog and want to pay for it, you could use:

- Typepad (with 30 day free trial): www.typepad.com
- Blog.com (upgrade): www.blog.com

If you want to stay informed about what's happening at all the blogs you like without having to visit them daily, you can use an RSS reader. This is a tool that watches all blogs and presents them to you in one overview. RSS readers are not limited to blogs only. News from every site that has a small (mostly orange) icon with RSS in it can be viewed in a RSS reader. Pretty useful! Some people claim that RSS readers and similar tools will replace traditional media because they let you personalize the available news. This is what is called "pulling" the news yourself instead of what is "pushed" by the traditional media.

Some free RSS readers are:

- Bloglines: www.bloglines.com
- Newsgator: www.newsgator.com (with the option to integrate the RSS reader in MS Outlook)

Why don't you start your own blog? It's free, easy and it helps to build visibility and trust.

# Chapter 7

# Follow up and stay in touch with your network

Making a first connection is one thing, but following up and keeping in touch with your network, is very difficult for most people. It is seen as an activity that can be done when there is some time left. But when do we have time "left" in this hectic era? In order to get our work done and have a balance between our personal and professional life we need to plan things carefully. The same applies to staying in touch with your network. It has to be an activity like any other on your to do list, and not the last one! Your network can help you realize the other things from your list faster and easier. Then you have to take action. It is your network and your responsibility to tap into its power.

## Follow up

I'm always surprised at how rarely people follow up. A survey of sales executives by the United States National Research Bureau, for example, found that "80% of all sales are made after the fifth call." However, nine out of ten sales people quit before they get that far. Persistence pays off, but few persist.

This doesn't only apply to sales, but also in relationship building. You don't have a relationship if you just met someone once.

How do you follow up? Many people tell me: "I don't know what to say in a follow up call or I don't know what to write in a follow up email."

If you read the previous chapters attentively, you know that there are many opportunities to reconnect with people after a first contact. Or a second, third, fourth...

As you know the first condition to do a good follow up is that you listen to people. Don't listen for your own direct business, but listen to how you can help them. Listen in order to get opportunities to follow up. Again, the basis of following up is listening how you can be of service to them. It is not about your products or services.

## Do what you promised to do

The best follow up action can be done when you already talked about how you can help the other person. If you made a promise please keep it, otherwise it will backfire on you. If you have troubles remembering or keeping promises, you better not make any. It is better that your contacts have no expectations than an expectation that is not fulfilled. If you made a promise, your logical follow-up action is to do that.

## Give

When you've listened carefully, there are several things you can do. Even without making a promise up front. Some of them are:

- Send an interesting article (extra special if you do it by regular mail and include a handwritten note)
- Point out a helpful website
- Share more info or tips about a subject you talked about
- Send some of your non-marketing material (see the part about "Giving" on page 64)
- Write or talk about the common ground you found in your previous conversations
- Send the contact data of someone who could be useful (see also the next tip)

- Introduce this person to someone from your network
- Introduce someone from your network to this person
- Refer someone from your network to this person
- Refer this person to someone from your network
- Remind the person of a promise she made to you

## Send your contact information in electronic format

This can be combined with another action or if you only had a very short talk and only exchanged business cards.

**Send an email with your Vcard.** Explicitly tell your contacts that you want to make their life easier by doing this.

You can also **send your Plaxo card** and encourage people who don't use Plaxo yet to start using it. Personalize your invitation to help them see the benefits for themselves.

A small warning about Vcards: when sending Vcards of your contacts make sure you delete confidential information, like the notes you made about this person. I once received a Vcard with detailed personal information about how they met on vacation and which other people were also involved. This was a bit too much information for me!

## Step into the Golden Triangle Cycle

After your first follow up undertaking and response from the other person, you step in the Golden Triangle cycle:

- If you gave something, you can ask for something else.
- If you received something, you can thank the person and/or give something in return.

- After the response you can do this again and again and again. With every cycle, you strengthen your relationship. It also gets easier to ask for the things you need.

## Ask about the information you gave

An alternative follow up action is to ask what happened with the information, introduction or referral you gave, or give something more. You always have something to talk about, and at the same time you remind the person about your first "good deed" without stating this explicitly.

## The frequency of a follow up

Research has shown that to build a relationship with (and to be remembered by) a person you have to keep this average frequency of contacts in mind:

- 1st contact
- 2nd contact: within 24 hours
- 3rd contact: within two weeks after second contact
- 4th contact: within a month after the third contact
- Then every six months

When you follow this frequency you will stay on top of your contact's mind, especially if you are always looking for ways you can give something to him.

Another important aspect of keeping in touch is that the (name of the) other person will be stored better in your own memory. This enhances the chance that you will remember his name next time you meet. This is important in building relationships. As a consequence, I don't recommend automating your follow up completely. Before any email or mail is sent to the people you want to build a personal relationship with, (re) read the content and look at the names. This will help you a lot!

## The result of a good follow up action

It is in our genes that when we receive something, we want to give something back. It depends in a substantial part how the other person values this "present," and it depends on how often you have given something. Your attitude is also important. People sense almost immediately when you give in order to get. In an extreme case, this becomes blackmailing and extortion.

Of course, you won't go that far. Keep in mind that when you give without expecting anything in return, this gives you more chances to get something. But you don't know what and when. You just have to trust the process. I can vouch that it really works. For example: I don't cold call anymore. Prospects call me because they heard about me via my network or I get introductions or referrals. The success rate of such a warm or hot call is in my case more than 90%!

## Difference between an introduction and a referral

In the previous chapters you already noticed that I make a distinction between an introduction and a referral. It is time to dig deeper into this matter.

Let's use a study by the Sandler Sales Institute to make things more clear.

The Sandler Sales Institute Study revealed that:

- Cold calls are successful 1% of the time
- Word of mouth is successful 15% of the time
- In case of a referral the success rate goes up to 50% of the time
- In case of a referral plus the person who made the referral either participates on the sales call or attends the meeting: the success rate goes up to 80% of the time!

Let's take a look at the figures and what they mean.

## Cold calls

- **What are they?** These are phone calls you make to people you know almost nothing about. You got the name of the organization from the Yellow Pages or from a list that you bought or rented. If you are lucky you also got the name of the person who you wanted to call.
- **Only 1% successful.** That's one of the reasons why almost nobody enjoys cold calling or prospecting. You are turned down so often that it can really get into your system. Note: they are not turning you down as a person; it's the reason why you are calling they say "no" to. So, don't take it personally!

## Word of mouth

- **What is it?** Word of mouth in this context means that people pass on information about you or your organization. Though this is a spontaneous act, this can be stimulated by "tell a friend" buttons on your website or "bring a friend to our store" actions.
- **Only 15% successful.** One of the reasons is that most people don't do this in an active way. If we are asked about an organization, a product, a service or a person, we will give our opinion. If we are enthusiastic, we will recommend them, but most of the time, we do not tend to do this proactively ourselves.

## Referral

- What is it? A referral is a very positive message about you or your organization whereby you are strongly recommended. The difference with word of mouth is that someone takes action to do this. This can be on her initiative or on your request.
- 50% successful. This is 50 times higher than a cold call, so this really works much better. The reason is that there is already a bond of trust between the

person who refers you and the third party. The stronger the bond between them, the higher the chance of success for you!

**Referral with participating intermediary**

- **What is it?** This is a referral whereby the connecting party actively participates in the "conversation." This can be during a conference call (or chat) or preferably in a face-to-face meeting that is set up by the intermediary, but it can also be done via email. See the next chapter about introducing people via email.
- **80% successful.** The reason is that the intermediary proactively connects the two other parties. This can be done not only on a business or professional level, but also on a personal level.

**Introduction** (not mentioned in the Sandler Sales Institute study)

- What is it? This is the action of connecting people. The message can contain a recommendation, but most of the time it is more an act to situate a person. In an "introduction" you pass on their Elevator Story in your words. In a "referral" you talk about your own experiences, you preferably tell your own story about both parties and make a recommendation. In other words, you can always make an introduction, even if you don't know one or both parties well. You only give a referral when you are convinced (and preferably have experienced) that the offer is good.
- 30% successful. This is my guess, not based on any study or figures. This success rate is higher than word of mouth thanks to the proactive action of introducing one person to another. This is lower than a referral because there is no bond of trust between the person who introduces and the one who gets introduced.

Introductions and referrals have a much higher success rate than cold calls or word of mouth publicity. This applies to your professional as well as to your personal life.

You need a network for introductions and referrals, so start today by making an inventory of your network (see also the exercises at the back of the book). You'll be surprised to find out how many people you know. If you think your network is too small, start building and expanding it. Don't forget to take action yourself and start introducing and referring people to each other.

***Networking success tip: Go through your contacts at least every month. This will give you new ideas for the projects your working on right now. At one time a name might attract your attention more than in another month. This might be a good moment to contact this person. Going through your contacts once a month will also help you from constantly going to the same people for advice.***

## Introduce two people via email

As I already stated, one of the most powerful ways to build and strengthen your network is to introduce and refer people to each other. I strongly recommend doing it as much as you can. It will strengthen your relationships and start "boomerang effects" you never could have dreamt of!

If you have a large network, how do you make sure you have time for other things aside from introducing and referring people?

Let me share with you how I use email to introduce two (or sometimes even more) network contacts of mine to each other.

## Introduce or refer a possible supplier and customer to each other

This is an (imaginary) example of an introduction or referral email:

To: eric.rogers@best-accountant-in-the-world.com
Cc: john.johnson@web-designer-number-one.com
Subject: introduction

*Hi Eric,*

*I want to introduce you to John Johnson (in cc). John is the Managing Director of Web Designer Number One. John may be the guy that can help you out with your new website. They make great websites (on their website www.web-designer-number-one.com you find lots of examples and references). I've known John for a while and even worked with him at ABC Company. One of the things I will always remember him by, is his ability to offer a solution that satisfies the needs of the customer while staying within the budget. He is really customer focused. I even recall him a few times recommending another solution or even another vendor if he thought it was in the interest of his customer. I definitely recommend him and his team!*

*John,*

*Eric Rogers is my accountant and also a personal friend. In fact, he is such a good accountant because he is more focused on people than on numbers! Eric is looking for a new website. Because of our joint experiences and the great job you did for Supermarket XYZ (I accidentally heard their Marketing Manager bragging about you at the last Chamber of Commerce meeting), I thought you might be the perfect candidate.*

*I suggest the two of you get together for a talk. Maybe you can do this combined with watching a soccer game? I understand the both of you are fans of Manchester United.*

*Eric, you can reach John at: (telephone number John)*

*John, you can reach Eric at: (telephone number Eric)*

*Good luck!*

*Jan*

Let's take a look at the "ingredients" of my introduction or referral email:

### Header

- To: the person who is the "receiver" of the product, services, help
- Cc: the person who is the "supplier" of the product, services, help
- Subject: "introduction": this makes very clear what this email is about

You can put more people in the "to" and "cc" field if that's appropriate. You can also put everybody in the "to" field, but for me this makes it easier to know who I introduced to whom. This is especially useful for your "follow up" or "stay in touch" actions.

### Body

- **First I address the receiver then I address the supplier.**
- I always give the reason for connecting the both of them.
- After addressing the receiver I always address the supplier so he knows **something about the receiver and especially about my relationship towards the receiver.** This makes it easier for him to find common ground, and to start the relationship on a much higher level than with a "cold call." In this example, I even go a bit further: I go to the "value" level. Both are very customer and people focused. This is a very strong basis to build a relationship on, especially when a third party with whom they both have a good relationship with points this out (which is me in this case).
- The same applies of course for the receiver with regard to the supplier.

- I include what I **appreciate** about the person, organization, product or service. This way I maintain and strengthen my relationship with every party. Even when there is no future interaction between them, the email was worth the effort as a "relationship building action."

- I also try to find **commonalities on another level other than the professional one.** In this case they share a passion for soccer and they even support the same team. There is an instant bond. This bond exists most of the time (remember the 6 degrees of proximity), but we don't always find it in a conversation because we didn't talk about the areas where we might be related. If you, as the connector, know about the interests that two people share then tell them. This way you help them to get a flying start.

- **Include other references and objective parties if possible.** The better the receiver knows them the better the reputation of the supplier. In this example I first referred to the references at the website of Web Designer Number One. Then I gave a second reference: the Marketing Manager of Supermarket XYZ.

**Conclusion:**

- **Call to action: I suggest that they contact each other**. This means:
    - THEY are expected to take ACTION, and there are no barriers to do this, because I (the respected and trusted third party) told them to do this.
    - I put the telephone number of the "supplier" first, because I want to encourage the "receiver" to make contact. This is more comfortable for the "supplier." This way I try to decrease the feeling of "selling" something as much as possible, and I open the possibilities of building a relationship and helping each other out.

- They contact EACH OTHER, not me anymore. I step out of the process. I did my part of the job: connecting them. Now it's up to them. This helps me to spend my time wisely as I'm not the intermediary anymore.

- **Telephone contact data:** so they can quickly reach each other. If they want to have contact via email, they already have it in the header of the email. I don't recommend following up on an introduction like this via email. The way is wide open for a personal contact via the telephone.

- **An alternative for the contact data is to include both people's Vcard.**

  - Pro: complete data, can directly be saved by both parties in their contact database or email program.

  - Con: when you keep notes on the people in your network, they are also in the Vcard you include in your email. However, there is a simple way around this: include the Vcard in your email, open it and delete the data you don't want to send. These changes will only be saved in the Vcard you send and not in your contacts database.

For some people this example might be perceived as too pushy. Please note that this is an email to two people you already know and have a good relationship with. In this case, I am very confident that bringing them together will be beneficial for both of them. Read further for an example of people you don't know that well.

## Make a general introduction or referral

If you are not a small business owner, freelancer or sales representative, you may ask yourself: how does the previous example apply to my situation?

Frankly, it is the same. You can always connect people like in the previous example. Helping your network is not only useful for the future, but it is also fun and very satisfying.

Let me give you one more example of people working in the same, large organization. If you work in a small organization, you're better off doing the introductions in person and face-to-face. Because of the scale of a small organization, this doesn't cost you much time or effort (no need to travel) and is more powerful.

The example of making an introduction within a large organization goes like this:

*To: Thomas.Hunter@company-abc.com*
*Cc: Sue.Allen@company-abc.com*
*Subject: introduction*

*Hi Thomas,*

*I want to introduce you to Sue Allen (in cc). Sue is one of the team members of the Eureca project. As you know, the Eureca project faced lots of challenges with legislation changing and some team members being moved to other countries. But you know the saying "a challenge is a way to grow." And that's exactly what happened to Sue. Sue got the daunting task to take over part of the project regarding legislation. And she did that really well! I experienced her knowledge myself when I had to deal with the local law in a number of Asian countries. Sue does know very much about this and has built a good network to support her. I definitely recommend her for your next project!*

*Sue,*

*Thomas Hunter is one of our international project leaders. I know he has had difficulty in the past finding the right people for his team with regard to local legislation. He is now assembling the team for his next project and I think your expertise will benefit this project. Thomas is a great man to work with. I enjoyed the way he leads his teams: he supports his team members in every way he can and encourages them to take responsibility. He is also very good at delegating decision power to his team members. As you know, I find this very important myself. In my opinion he is one of the best project leaders of our company.*

*In addition to a possible professional match, you will have lots to talk about your shared passion for winter holidays and more specifically snowboarding.*

*I suggest the two of you get together for a talk.*

*Thomas, you can reach Sue at: (telephone number Sue)*

*Sue, you can reach Thomas at: (telephone number Thomas)*

*Good luck!*

*Jan*

You see that it is not that difficult to introduce or refer people via email. Make a habit of doing this yourself!

## When to write an introduction or referral email?

The correct answer is: as often as possible. Every introduction or referral is a very powerful relationship seed. It is way more powerful than passing on information (but don't stop doing this!). The more those seeds you plant, the more flowers can grow. Flowers that carry many more seeds for you.

But again there has to be a balance between quantity and quality. It makes **no sense to keep introducing and referring people and organizations if:**

- You are **not sure about the quality they provide.** Beware of this situation because you don't want to jeopardize your existing relationships.
- You are always **choosing the same people as "receivers" of the introduction.** They have a saturation point, too. They have better work to do than connecting with the people you introduce them to. You want to keep your reputation high. If people get too many introductions they begin to wonder about the quality, and they begin to wonder if you have no business to take care of yourself.

- **You ask money for being the matchmaker.** This has to be clear for both parties. An unconditional referral is much more powerful and more credible. Again, the question about quality arises for the receiver if you get commissions for connecting people.

Only connect people if you know that they are both open for this contact. Therefore, you should always think of WIFM (What's In For Me) for both parties. Always point out the win-win situation.

## Why email instead of a phone call, a letter or in person?

Introducing or referring people by phone, letter of via a face-to-face contact is one of the most powerful actions that you can do – sometimes more powerful than email. But I still prefer email because of the following reasons:

- **Less time consuming.**
  - Personally, I type rather fast, so it doesn't take lots of time.
  - One email to all parties. I don't have to call them both, or invite them both at the same time in a conference call or group chat. But if you want to do that: Skype (www.skype.com) and MSN Messenger (messenger.msn.com) are excellent tools to communicate with your network one-on-one or in a group.
- **I do it whenever it suits ME,** I don't need any other person to be available at the same time. Short breaks between meetings, projects or tasks are ideal moments to type an introduction or referral email.
- **It is written.** This is "proof " of the introduction or referral. Any party can come back to the email. The person who is introduced can use the email to make a follow up call, and I also have something I can bring up in a "contact maintenance" (or follow up) conversation.

- **Instant credibility for both parties.** They can "ride" on the waves of trust that already exists between them and me.
- **It gives me the opportunity to strengthen the relationship with both of them.** Not only with the person that is introduced, but also with the person I make the introduction to. I always make sure to explain the qualities, competences or expertise of both persons. This is a kind of "public appraisal." Public praise that is concrete and specific is one of the most powerful relationship building tools.

Did you already get a public praise or introduction via email in the way I describe it? If you did, you will agree with me that it makes you feel good. If you want other people to feel good, be sure to include a "public praise." This also helps you to get more from these emails. Lead by example! A big warning though: be sincere, realistic and factual. People don't believe you if you only write in superlatives. Mean what you write otherwise this will have an opposite effect. Be generous and write lots of introduction and referral emails, but watch out with the superlatives.

## What about people you don't know very well?

If you don't know the person well, clearly mention this in your email. Always state your relationship with both parties. Tell them where you met, whether you already did business and whether you have a personal experience with one or both of them. This will not only make the situation more clear for both of them and give them more things to find common ground, but will also keep your relationships good.

Let's look at the example of John and Eric again, but this time you only met John yesterday evening at a reception at the Chamber of Commerce.

You could write something like this:

*Eric, I want to introduce you to John. I met John yesterday at an event of the Chamber of Commerce. He is a web designer. I don't know of his work, but he apparently knows his business and has some nice references (look on his website: www.web-designer-number-one.com).*

*John, I want to introduce you to Eric. Eric is my accountant and in the meantime a personal friend. He wants to have a new website. After our talk yesterday I got the feeling that you might be one of the candidates for the job.*

*I suggest that you contact each other. These are the telephone numbers:...*

*Good luck!*

*Jan*

In this example I make clear that:

- I don't know anything about the quality of John's work. So, I don't give a referral, but an introduction. Eric knows he must qualify John himself. He knows that I can't give any guarantees and doesn't expect that from me.
- I clearly state to John that I have a personal relationship with Eric. I also state clearly that John is not my number one, but one of many candidates. He knows that I take a risk by introducing him to Eric, a personal friend. He knows that when he screws up, I will lose face. This is a strong sign of trust towards him. This may sound odd to you, but many of us are very sensitive to this. This is the reason why many sales people have "cold call" fear: not being liked as a person and jeopardizing the human relationship.

Think of this example when you introduce two people to each other. Make sure the personal relationships and reason for contact are clear for all parties.

## How to react when somebody asks you for an introduction or referral?

If you know the person well and you are convinced about her qualities, then you will probably have no objection referring her, especially if you don't have to spend much time doing this, using the email technique I described.

But what if:

- Your relationship with the person she wants to be introduced to is not good or very basic
- You don't know the person asking for a referral well
- You do know the person asking for a referral, but are not convinced of the quality
- You do know the person asking for a referral, but don't approve of the way of contacting people (this is especially the case nowadays when using networking websites like LinkedIn)

In these cases we experience dual feelings. We hesitate to make the introduction because we don't want to jeopardize our existing relationship, and we don't want to "kill" the relationship with the person asking for an introduction or referral either. Many people have difficulty "letting other people down" and saying "no." If you find yourself in a similar situation, you might benefit from the following tips.

| **Relationship with person asking for an introduction** | **Relationship with person she wants to be connected with** | **Action** |
|---|---|---|
| Good | Good | Connect them! |
| Good | Not Good | Honestly say that your relationship is not good and that you're not the best contact to reach this person. In some cases, it is also good to warn about any past experiences with this person. But be objective. |
| Good | Don't know her yet | Honestly say that you don't know this person well yet. Maybe you want to find out more or do business with this person yourself before you "open your gate" to this contact. Say this and also say in what time frame you think you should be contacted again with the referral in question. |

| Relationship with person asking for an introduction | Relationship with person she wants to be connected with | Action |
|---|---|---|
| Don't know her yet | Good | Tell her honestly that you don't know her well enough. Also, tell what she should do to make you more comfortable and to build trust. |
| Don't know her yet | Not Good | See previous point. In this case, it might be too soon to mention your "bad" relationship with the person that she wants to be introduced to. |
| Not Good | | Does this person know about this? Apparently not, because he is still asking you for an introduction. Most people don't do this when the relationship is bad. However awkward this may be, this is a good time to talk about your relationship. Explain why you have a "bad feeling." Be objective and use facts and figures. Listen to the other person. If he is still willing to continue this "relationship," tell him what you need to build trust again and how much time you probably are going to need. |
| Doubts about quality | | This situation is not as bad as the previous one. In this case most of the time you like this person one way or the other. It is more the "technical" part of the deal that you are concerned about.<br>Say this honestly and build your statement with facts and figures. Tell her what you would like to see changed, and under which conditions you are willing to make the connection. |
| Doubts about ways of contacting people | | This is a special note concerning the use of networking websites like LinkedIn (www.linkedin.com). Tell the other person that this is another medium of communication, but that the same rules of making contact still apply. See also tips about online networking etiquette. |

## Asking for introductions and referrals yourself

The previous table also applies to you when you are the one asking for an introduction or referral. Before doing this, always ask yourself what your relationship with the connector is and what his relationship with your desired contact is. If you are not sure, check it when you contact him.

Asking for referrals is best done via a more personal medium like telephone or face-to-face contact. Why?

- You can check about your relationship with the connector and his relationship with your desired contact.
- You can explain why you want to have this referral. Explain why this is a win-win situation for both the third party (especially the third party!) and yourself.
- You can go into the details of your request. You can teach him how to make the best referral, (how to tell your Elevator Story) and maybe you can learn from him how to approach this person once the connection is made. Ask for common ground so you can have an interesting conversation.

Of course, the way of asking for referrals depends on the nature of your request and of the business you're in, but when you are trying to reach "Mr. Big Shot" within or outside your organization, this is definitely the approach you need.

## When to use which communication medium

Nowadays there are lots of communication media that enable us to keep in touch with our network: face-to-face conversation, telephone (land, mobile and over the Internet), email, letters, SMS, instant messaging, chatting, forums and messaging via websites, tele- and videoconferencing. We also see these communication media being integrated in appliances like mobile phones. More and more media and supporting hardware are converging.

So, in this world where we can communicate 7 days a week and 24 hours a day, which medium do we use for what occasion?

Here are some general rules:

- **Email: is good for non-urgent, informative matters, for sending documents and for making introductions.** Don't use it to solve problems. Many people hide behind email to avoid confrontation.

  I once worked as manager of the project department for a software company that developed its own software. My department had the daunting task to configure and implement the software for the customers. Inevitably, there were always some small bugs or problems that needed to be fixed. One day one of my team members had been sending emails back and forth to a customer to resolve a problem all morning. When I asked whether he already telephoned the other guy, he said he didn't. It was clearly a case of "hiding behind the keyboard" and being afraid of the confrontation. So, I strongly suggested picking up the phone. Within 10 minutes the problem was clear and half an hour later he solved it. Instead of being angry the customer was very happy to have a solution. My team member had been afraid for nothing.

  This happens a lot. We begin to imagine things and make up worst-case scenarios, and then "hide behind the keyboard." It takes time to write emails, and more importantly the more text, the more danger for misinterpretation. We miss the tone of voice and the emotion of the other person and this frequently causes misinterpretation. So, be careful when to use email and when not.

  If you want more tips about email use, you can subscribe to the weekly email tip of Timesmart: www.time-smart.com/subscribe-tip/default.htm

- **Letters.** Do you like to open your mailbox nowadays? Most people don't.

Because 90% of the letters they receive are bills and (unsolicited) publicity. All the good stuff comes via email. So, what can we learn from this? Letters are almost never used anymore, but we are still happy to receive them (if they contain good news). So, why don't you send a letter to your network from time to time?

It is **really appreciated** because:

1. Almost nobody sends letters anymore, so you **stand out from the crowd.**
2. You took the time to write a letter, sign it, write the address on the envelope, put a stamp on it and take it to the mailbox. Email takes less effort. You will be **perceived as a person who goes the extra mile for his network and as a consequence you get the reputation of being a valuable contact.**

- **Postcards.** Everybody likes to receive a postcard, and it's not much work. It's less than a letter, but still more than an email. This will make you stand out from the crowd, and it's also relatively cheap. Another advantage of a funny or special postcard is that many people put them on the announcement board or stick it to the wall of their office. You get more visibility and will be remembered!
- **Telephone: used to make appointments, solve problems and have a real conversation when it's not possible to see each other face-to-face.** Nowadays it's becoming cheaper and even free to call somebody else. Skype (www.skype.com) for example, enables you to call for free via the Internet, even with several people at once.
- **Face-to-face:** there is no substitute for the "real stuff." Although there are exceptions (for example, online networking guru, Scott Allen started a business together with someone he never met in person), **experiencing the other person "as a whole" is almost always necessary to get a good and lasting relationship.**

If it's really true that your words only count for 7%, your voice for 28% and your body language for 65% then it's absolutely necessary to meet each other face-to-face from time to time. This is a real challenge for international organizations with virtual teams from all around the world that have to work together. In my opinion, it is necessary to meet each other, preferably at the start of a project, face-to-face, and also to get to know each other on both levels: work experience and personal situation. These two levels are necessary to really trust someone in the work place

- **Online networking:** this is a rather new medium, but a very strong one, with its own characteristics. You already read how to deal with this in the previous chapter.

My golden tip about communication media is: use the preferred medium of the person who you want to get in touch with. Not the medium you prefer yourself. This is also an example of "Give and Receive." You use their favorite medium (you give) and they will provide you faster with an (better) answer (you receive).

You might recognize the following situation. I was trying to reach a contact of mine via the telephone, but he didn't answer. I left a voice message on the land and the mobile phone, but didn't get an answer back. Then I sent an email. Within the minute I got a response! He definitely is an "email person." So, if I want him to do something for me, I better take his preference into account.

Another example: some friends of mine are very "into SMS." They are so used to sending text messages via their mobile phones, they even don't have to look at the device anymore to type a new message. Trying to call them is a case that is lost in advance, but when I send an SMS, I get my answer almost immediately.

Though I'm not a fan of SMS or sending emails back and forth if I want to arrange an appointment, I learned to adapt to the preferences of the people from my network, and this works best. If you want something from them, play on their terms.

However, this doesn't mean that you have to neglect your own needs. If their way of communication is really difficult for you, you should speak up and work something out with them, and really do this, because networking is all about listening and communicating!

# Afterword

Only a small percentage of the people on this planet read books to improve their life. Even less (5%) do something with what they have read. These 5% are the people who are most successful in their personal and professional lives. Before you think of Bill Gates or Michael Schumacher and tell yourself you can't be as successful as they are and give up before you even get started, consider my definition of success.

***Success is the way you live up to your own expectations of life.***

Success is different for everybody. The best way to reach your own success is to do it step by step. Set yourself small goals. Chop a big challenge in small pieces, and then do them one by one. I presented you examples and practical tips. I also took the time to explain why some tips work and why others don't. I did it this way because I wanted to inspire you to find your own networking way.

If you apply a step-by-step approach to this book, you can pick one tip and do it. Just do it. It doesn't have to be perfect the first time. Just take the first step and you will see that it becomes easier while you are walking on the networking path.

If you don't feel comfortable doing this, just know that you are not alone. I have read many books and was delighted with what I learned, but really bringing these insights into practice and integrating them in my life, was and is something completely different. Just take the steps one at a time and you will find that it becomes easier and easier.

If you're like me, you have read the whole book without doing the exercises and without visiting the websites I mentioned. At this point you have read the whole book, so now is a good time to start all over again and/or pick the things you feel that are the most important for you to bring into practice. Do it. Then, after a couple of weeks or months, read this book again. You will see that other things will look more important to you. Maybe you'll ask yourself, "How could I have overlooked this brilliant tip the first time?"

This is very normal. In the time frame between now and the time you read this book again, you have experienced several things and probably became more aware about networking. You learned from your experiences and became a better networker. So, the next time you read this book, you can go the next level. You will keep improving every time by bringing the tips more and more into practice. By the time you run out of ideas, I hopefully will have written my next book.

A last word: don't forget to enjoy your networking journey. Have fun with the people you encounter, be grateful for what you receive and enjoy giving without expecting anything in return. It will come back to you in one way or the other!

Have a great networking life!

Jan

PS: If you really did try one or more of the tips from this book and want to share your experience with me, you can send me an email: jan.vermeiren@networking-coach.com

PS2: If you really enjoyed the book and improved your professional or personal life and want to thank me, you can help me to help others. Look at my website www.networking-coach.com for the charities I support. If you want to support them, too, you can make a donation to these charities yourself or via me.

# Exercises

In this chapter you find a few exercises that will help you to get more insight in yourself and in your network. Fill in your Network Plan, including your Elevator Story. By doing the exercises and filling in your network plan it will allow you to network more effectively and more efficiently. In short, this will allow you to tap into the tremendous power of your network.

## Values Discovery Exercise

It's not always easy to tell people right away what your values are. That's why I do a small exercise in my networking courses to find your six most important values. It goes as follows:

1. Write the values from the table below on small pieces of paper.
2. Go through the stack of small papers and make two new piles.
   a. Left: the values that appeal to you right away.
   b. Right: the values that don't appeal to you right away. If you hesitate, put the value on the right pile. It won't make it through the rest of the process.
3. Take the left pile and place the first six papers in front of you.
4. Then go through the rest of the values of the left pile, one by one. Evaluate if the value on the paper in your hand, is more important to you than one of the six values in front of you.
   a. If it is not more important than one of the six in front of you, put the paper on the right pile.

b. If it is more important than one of the six values in front of you, replace that paper with the one in your hand. Then put the value you hold in your hand now on the right pile.

5. Go through the whole pile until you have only six values left. These are your most important values.

If you feel that writing the values on cards is a barrier for you, you can consider copying this page and doing the elimination exercise by striking through the values that least appeal to you till you only have six left. You can do this right away in the book, but then I advise you to use a pencil so you can use an eraser if you want to do the exercise again.

***Note:*** this doesn't mean that the other values are not important. It only means that they are less important than the six that were left at the end of the exercise. Why six? Because this is a good number to work with in practice.

This is not only a good exercise to help you gain more insight in yourself, but also to communicate with others about your values. It can be quite revealing when you do this exercise with your life partner, kids, colleagues, business partners and other network contacts!

**Values**

| | | | |
|---|---|---|---|
| Abundance | Alertness | Availability | Brilliance |
| Acceptance | Altruism | Awareness | Calmness |
| Accomplishment | Ambition | Awe | Camaraderie |
| Accuracy | Amusement | Balance | Candor |
| Achievement | Anticipation | Beauty | Capability |
| Acknowledgement | Appreciation | Being the best | Care |
| Activeness | Assertiveness | Belonging | Carefulness |
| Adaptability | Assurance | Benevolence | Celebrity |
| Adoration | Attentiveness | Bliss | Certainty |
| Adventure | Attractiveness | Boldness | Challenge |
| Affection | Audacity | Bravery | Charity |

| | | | |
|---|---|---|---|
| Charm | Depth | Extravagance | Humility |
| Cheerfulness | Desire | Extroversion | Humor |
| Clarity | Determination | Fairness | Hygiene |
| Cleanliness | Devotion | Faith | Imagination |
| Cleverness | Dignity | Fame | Impact |
| Closeness | Direction | Fascination | Independence |
| Comfort | Directness | Fidelity | Industry |
| Commitment | Discipline | Financial | Inspiration |
| Compassion | Discovery | independence | Integrity |
| Concentration | Discretion | Firmness | Intelligence |
| Confidence | Diversity | Fitness | Intensity |
| Conformity | Dominance | Flexibility | Intimacy |
| Congruency | Dreaming | Flow | Introversion |
| Connection | Drive | Fluency | Intuition |
| Consciousness | Duty | Focus | Inventiveness |
| Consistency | Dynamism | Freedom | Investing |
| Contentment | Eagerness | Friendliness | Joy |
| Continuity | Economy | Fun | Justice |
| Contribution | Ecstasy | Gallantry | Kindness |
| Control | Education | Generosity | Knowledge |
| Conviction | Effectiveness | Gentility | Leadership |
| Conviviality | Efficiency | Giving | Learning |
| Coolness | Elegance | Grace | Liveliness |
| Cooperation | Empathy | Gratitude | Logic |
| Cordiality | Encouragement | Growth | Love |
| Correctness | Energy | Guidance | Loyalty |
| Courage | Enjoyment | Happiness | Making a |
| Courtesy | Entertainment | Harmony | difference |
| Creativity | Enthusiasm | Health | Mastery |
| Credibility | Excellence | Helpfulness | Maturity |
| Curiosity | Excitement | Heroism | Modesty |
| Daring | Experience | Honesty | Motivation |
| Decisiveness | Expertise | Honor | Mysteriousness |
| Delight | Exploration | Hopefulness | Nerve |
| Dependability | Expressiveness | Hospitality | Obedience |

| | | | |
|---|---|---|---|
| Open-mindedness | Professionalism | Serenity | Traditionalism |
| Optimism | Prosperity | Service | Trust |
| Order | Prudence | Sexuality | Trustworthiness |
| Organization | Punctuality | Sharing | Truth |
| Originality | Purity | Significance | Understanding |
| Passion | Realism | Silence | Uniqueness |
| Peace | Reason | Silliness | Unity |
| Perceptiveness | Reasonableness | Simplicity | Usefulness |
| Perfection | Recognition | Sincerity | Utility |
| Persistence | Reflection | Solidarity | Variety |
| Persuasiveness | Relaxation | Solitude | Victory |
| Philanthropy | Reliability | Spirituality | Virtue |
| Playfulness | Resourcefulness | Spontaneity | Vision |
| Pleasantness | Respect | Stability | Vitality |
| Pleasure | Rest | Strength | Warmth |
| Popularity | Sacrifice | Structure | Watchfulness |
| Power | Satisfaction | Success | Wealth |
| Pragmatism | Security | Support | Winning |
| Precision | Self-control | Surprise | Wisdom |
| Preparedness | Selflessness | Sympathy | Wonder |
| Presence | Self-reliance | Synergy | Youthfulness |
| Privacy | Sensitivity | Teamwork | |
| Pro-activity | Sensuality | Timeliness | |

## Your current network

Networking effectively (doing the right things) and efficiently (doing the things right) starts with an inventory of your current network.

Depending on your point of view there are different networks and different people in those networks. It makes a difference if you look at your network from a personal point of view or a professional one. Your professional view will depend on what kind of function you have. Are you self-employed? Or do you work for a multinational? Do you work in sales or do you primarily interact with your colleagues inside your organization?

## Exercises

The next exercise will help you to get you started and to inspire you. The list below is only the tip of the iceberg. Expand it according to your own situation, needs and wishes.

The exercise goes as follows: look at the list and fill each row with the best person you can imagine. Evaluate afterwards:

- Are those people really the best? If not, do you need other names? Yes? Then start by asking your network who they can recommend.
- Are there any blanks? If so, do you feel that it is important for you to fill this row? Yes? Then start by asking your network who they can recommend.

Having this list will ensure you that you have the names of the best people that can help you at all times. Don't wait to make this list until you need it desperately. Do it now, at a moment you don't need it. Chances are that you won't remember the names of the best people when you are in an "emergency" situation, especially when you don't have regular contact with them.

Extra tip: this list can be another "low cost, high perceived value" item. When people are urgently looking for a solution to their problem they will be very grateful if you can present them the names of the best people you know.

### Professional list

Chances are that you don't need all the people in this list right away. Keep in mind that they can be excellent sources of information and new contacts. It's not only important who you know, but also who they know!

| Service/Profession | Name | Telephone Number | Remarks |
|---|---|---|---|
| Accountant | | | |
| Handyman (for repairs) | | | |

# Let's Connect!

| Service/Profession | Name | Telephone Number | Remarks |
|---|---|---|---|
| Computer Help | | | |
| Lawyer | | | |
| Telephone Company | | | |
| Realtor | | | |
| Taxi Service | | | |
| Pizza Delivery | | | |
| Restaurant Breakfast | | | |
| Restaurant Lunch | | | |
| Restaurant Dinner | | | |
| Café/Pub | | | |
| Gift Shop | | | |
| Banker | | | |
| Chamber of Commerce | | | |
| Cleaning Team | | | |
| College or University Staff | | | |
| Hotel Manager | | | |

| Service/Profession | Name | Telephone Number | Remarks |
|---|---|---|---|
| Personnel Professional | | | |
| Insurance Agent | | | |
| Lobbyist | | | |
| Office Supplies | | | |
| Printer | | | |
| Security Guard | | | |
| Travel Agent | | | |
| Interim Agency | | | |
| Head Hunter | | | |
| Local Politician | | | |
| Journalist | | | |
| Marketing Consultant | | | |
| Environmental Specialist | | | |

## Personal list

This is not only a handy list for yourself, but also for your spouse or kids when you are on vacation or for a nice present for newcomers in your community.

# Let's Connect!

| Service/Profession | Name | Telephone Number | Remarks |
|---|---|---|---|
| Police | | | |
| Doctor | | | |
| Dentist | | | |
| Hospital | | | |
| Accountant | | | |
| Auto Repair | | | |
| Baby Sitting | | | |
| Handyman (for repairs) | | | |
| Computer Help | | | |
| Dry Cleaning | | | |
| Electrician | | | |
| Gardener | | | |
| Housecleaner | | | |
| Lawyer | | | |
| Telephone Company | | | |
| Plumber | | | |

## Exercises

| Service/Profession | Name | Telephone Number | Remarks |
|---|---|---|---|
| Realtor | | | |
| Taxi Service | | | |
| Supermarket | | | |
| Pizza Delivery | | | |
| Restaurant Breakfast | | | |
| Restaurant Lunch | | | |
| Restaurant Dinner | | | |
| Café/Pub | | | |
| Bakery | | | |
| Banker | | | |
| Insurance Agent | | | |
| Travel Agent | | | |
| School Kindergarten | | | |

Review and update these lists once a year so you always can contact them when you need them!

## Let's Connect!

### Your networks

We are all part of several networks, but don't always realize this. In my training courses many people get a real feeling of how small the world is when we do a small brainstorming about the different networks we're part of.

These are some examples. Find three names of people for every network. If you can't find three names, this might be a network you want to expand in a proactive way!

| Network | Names |
|---|---|
| 1 Family | Name 1:<br>Name 2:<br>Name 3: |
| 2 Friends | Name 1:<br>Name 2:<br>Name 3: |
| 3 Neighbors | Name 1:<br>Name 2:<br>Name 3: |
| 4 Sports and/or Hobby | Name 1:<br>Name 2:<br>Name 3: |
| 5 School/Alumni | Name 1:<br>Name 2:<br>Name 3: |
| 6 Politics | Name 1:<br>Name 2:<br>Name 3: |

| Network | Names |
|---|---|
| 7 Religion | Name 1:<br>Name 2:<br>Name 3: |
| 8 Media | Name 1:<br>Name 2:<br>Name 3: |
| 9 Direct Colleagues | Name 1:<br>Name 2:<br>Name 3: |
| 10 Colleagues from Other Departments | Name 1:<br>Name 2:<br>Name 3: |
| 11 Customers | Name 1:<br>Name 2:<br>Name 3: |
| 12 Suppliers | Name 1:<br>Name 2:<br>Name 3: |
| 13 Partnerships | Name 1:<br>Name 2:<br>Name 3: |
| 14 Conculleagues (positive word for competition) | Name 1:<br>Name 2:<br>Name 3: |
| 15 Labor Union | Name 1:<br>Name 2:<br>Name 3: |

## Let's Connect!

| Network | Names |
|---|---|
| 16 Consultants | Name 1:<br>Name 2:<br>Name 3: |
| 17 Trainers | Name 1:<br>Name 2:<br>Name 3: |
| 18 Government | Name 1:<br>Name 2:<br>Name 3: |
| 19 Trade Organization Members | Name 1:<br>Name 2:<br>Name 3: |
| 20 Professional Organization Members | Name 1:<br>Name 2:<br>Name 3: |
| 21 Network and/or Service Club Members | Name 1:<br>Name 2:<br>Name 3: |
| 22 Financial Institutions (bank, insurance, venture capital...) | Name 1:<br>Name 2:<br>Name 3: |
| 23 Mentors and/or Coaches | Name 1:<br>Name 2:<br>Name 3: |

Keep in mind that this is just the tip of the iceberg. You know lots of people via other ways:

- Via your partner
- Via your children
- Via all the networks you belonged to in the past: old friends, previous work, high school…

It IS a small world. So, don't limit yourself and start giving, asking and thanking your current and past network!

## Networking successes

People help each other the whole time, but sometimes we forget that those things happened or we find it so natural that we forget to thank the people that helped us.

In the next two exercises you will focus on the help you received from your network.

### Past networking successes

In this exercise you focus on what people did for you in the past. This can be on a personal or professional level.

| Occasion | Name of person who helped me | What did he/she do? | How did I thank him/her? | Last moment of contact |
|---|---|---|---|---|
| | | | | |
| | | | | |
| | | | | |
| | | | | |
| | | | | |

If you forgot to thank the person, remember that it is never too late to thank somebody. You can still do it now. Even if you did thank the person, but your last contact is from a long time ago, this can be a good reason to contact this person again.

### Networking successes

This exercise is more focused on the future. During the next week, write down which people helped you (during this week) and how they did it. Also, write down how you thanked them or how you are going to thank them. Don't forget that you can always offer your expertise and your network contacts as a "thank you" gift!

| Occasion | Name of person who helped me | What did he/she do? | How did I thank him/her? |
|---|---|---|---|
| | | | |
| | | | |
| | | | |
| | | | |
| | | | |

Other exercises: if you have a commercial profile or run your own business, you can find lots of other interesting exercises in the books of Ivan Misner, especially in *"Business by Referral."* A recommendation!

# Your own networking plan

On the next pages I offer you a "networking plan" template. This is one of the tools that are used in my training courses to really take action. In this plan you basically summarize what you are going to do with the knowledge you acquired by reading this book. Fill this template in and take action. That's the only way the power of networking is going to benefit you!

This template is designed to be used for one goal in your professional or personal life. You can also use one template for multiple goals. However, the danger is that you will focus on one or two specific goals and not do the exercise for the other goals. As a consequence, you probably won't succeed in reaching these other goals.

Background information for filling in the networking plan

- *Passion:* always think of this passion when talking to people. People who speak with passion appeal to others. The energy of passion is contagious and will help you to build better relationships faster.
- *Values:* your six most important values (see also the "Values Discovery Exercise" on page 241). They can be used as criteria to decide where, when and with whom you are going to network.
- *Personal goal:* can either be professional or personal. When you do this exercise for the first time I advise you to go for a short-term goal and not make it too difficult on yourself. This way you can experience the power of networking. This first success will encourage you to keep involving your network to reach your goals. A goal should be SMART (see the tips about "Goals" on page 34).

- *People who are the best to help me reach this goal:* The column "Added Value" means: why do you choose this person and not somebody else? What special abilities, skills or contacts does this person have?
- *Where will I go?* events, organizations, receptions, fairs, parties...
- *What do I have to offer?* For ideas see "Giving" on page 64
- *Example of expertise on a professional level:* stories and examples are remembered better than anything else. Having an example will give you confidence.
- *Example of results of networking in the past:* this will remind you of the benefits of networking when you have a moment of de-motivation. This is also a great conversation piece.
- *My introduction:* a short message to get people to remember you and to ask questions.
- *Ingredients of my Elevator Stories:* keywords that you can use when you present yourself in different occasions (for guidelines see page 112).
- *I'm going to contact these people:* this will get you into action.
- *Which actions?* which tips from this book or ideas you got from reading this book are you going to put into practice?

# Networking Plan

**My passion**

**My values**

**One of my personal goals (professional or personal)**

**The best people for helping me reach this goal.**

| Name | Kind of relationship | Added Value |
|---|---|---|
| | | |
| | | |
| | | |
| | | |
| | | |
| | | |

# Let's Connect!

**Where will I go networking to reach my goal or to meet people that can help me reach my goal?**

**What do I have to offer?**

- **Within the organization I work for**

- **Outside the organization I work for**

**This is an example of my expertise on a professional level (in a few keywords). (This will help you in your networking conversations.)**

# Networking Plan

**This is an example of how networking did work for me in the past (in a few keywords). (This means an example of somebody helping you or you helping another person).**

**My introduction (seven to nine seconds):**

**These are the ingredients of my Elevator Stories:**

- **Professional**

- **Personal**

## Let's Connect!

**I'm going to contact these people:**

- **Someone who doesn't belong to my network yet:**

- **Someone I didn't talk to in a while (on a professional level):**

- **Someone I didn't talk to in a while (on a personal level):**

**How will I start networking? Which actions am I going to take? What am I going to do different at network events? What am I going to do different via online networking?**

# Used terms

- **6 degrees of proximity:** everybody is connected with anybody else in the world via six steps. Also called "6 degrees of separation."
- **Blog:** abbreviation of "weblog." Mostly it is defined as an online journal, which is published frequently (often daily). Readers can post comments on each journal entry.
- **Business Card Holder:** a small case the size of a standard business card. Used to store your own business cards and those of the people you meet.
- **Business Card Reader:** a small scanner that can be used to transform a paper business card to an electronic datasheet. Normally comes with Optical Character Recognition (OCR) software and is suited for most email software and common spreadsheets like MS Excel.
- **Conculleague:** a more positive word for competitor. In a world where "competing" companies work together (like the Ford-Mazda alliance, Wayne Baker describes in "Networking Smart") and more and more people and organizations start to focus on their own strengths instead of looking at the competition, the term "conculleague" seems more appropriate to use from now on.
- **Conference call:** a telephone call with several people involved. This can be from several locations within one company, between companies and from anywhere in the world. You can use free Internet telephone technology like Skype (www.skype.com) for a conference call.
- **eCourse:** a course via email. The idea behind most eCourses is that you receive small chunks of information at regular time intervals to optimize learning and apply the information you get.

- **eZine:** a magazine sent via email.
- **Give and Receive attitude:** giving without expecting anything in return. You will receive things in return, more than you expected, but you don't know when and from whom.
- **Golden triangle of networking:** giving, asking and thanking.
- **Grooming:** the way you take care of yourself. This not only involves clothing, but also your hair, fingernails, deodorant, teeth...Grooming is about your overall appearance.
- **Group chat:** a conversation via an instant messaging (free) tool like MSN Messenger or Yahoo Messenger with several people.
- **Instant Messaging:** real time exchange of messages via instant messaging tools like MSN Messenger (www.msnmessenger.com), Yahoo Messenger (messenger.yahoo.com), AOL Instant Messenger (www.aim.com), ICQ (www.icq.com) or Jabber (www.jabber.org). Skype (www.skype.com) can also be used for instant messaging.
- **Offline:** communication "in real life" as opposed to communication via the Internet. "Offline (networking) events" are events where you can meet people face-to-face as opposed to from behind a computer.
- **Online:** communication via the Internet. Online networking is networking via the Internet.
- **P2P or Peer-to-peer communication:** communication from one PC to another one. Examples of software that use this kind of technology are instant messaging tools like MSN Messenger and Yahoo Messenger, free Internet telephone technology like Skype and music exchange software like Kazaa.
- **RSS:** abbreviation of Rich Site Summary or Really Simple Syndication. It is an easy way to transfer information to applications like RSS Readers. With an RSS reader you can make a selection of websites from which you want

information. This is displayed in one overview. When there is new information from one or more websites this is automatically updated. So, you don't have to visit all the different websites anymore. Mostly used for blogs and news websites.

- **Skype (www.skype.com):** free telephone over the Internet. You can also call to mobile telephones at a lower cost than normal telecom operators offer.
- **SPAM:** unwanted emails (or other forms of communication).
- **URL:** abbreviation of "Uniform Resource Locator." Mostly used to describe the name of a website. For example, the URL of the website of the Networking Coach is: www.networking-coach.com.
- **Vcard:** contact data in an electronic format like the "contact data card" in email software like MS Outlook, Outlook Express or Lotus Notes.
- **WIFM:** What's In It For Me. It's a human tendency to think about yourself first. If you can avoid thinking about yourself first and instead find out what the other person wants and offer a benefit for him, you will build successful relationships.

# References and Recommended reading

## *Books*


- ALLEN SCOTT and TETEN DAVID, 2005, *The Virtual Handshake,* Amacom
- BAKER WAYNE, 2000, *Networking Smart,* Backinprint.com
- BURG BOB, 1994, *Endless Referrals,* McGraw-Hill
- CARNEGIE DALE, 1981, *How to Win Friends and Influence People,* Simon & Schuster
- CHOPRA DEEPAK, 1995, *The Seven Spiritual Laws of Success,* New World Library
- CONARD GEERT, 2005, *A Girlfriend in Every City,* Ecademy Press
- COVEY STEPHEN, 2004, *Seven Habits of Highly Effective People,* Free Press
- CROSS ROB and PARKER ANDREW, 2004, *The Hidden Power of Social Networks,* Harvard Business School Press
- CSIKSZENTMIHALYI MIHALY, 1991, *Flow,* Harper Perennial
- DARLING DIANE, 2003, *The Networking Survival Guide,* McGraw- Hill
- DE BRUIN CEES, 2005, *The Monkey Trap,* eBook
- FERAZZI KEITH, 2005, *Never Eat Alone,* Currency Doubleday
- FISHER DONNA and VILAS SANDY, 2000, *Power Networking,* Bard Press
- FISHER DONNA, 1995, *People Power,* Bard Press
- FISHER DONNA, 2002, *Professional Networking For Dummies,* Addison Wesley

- FRISHMAN RICK and LUBLIN JILL, 2004, *Networking Magic,* Adams Media Corporation
- GIOVAGNOLI MELISSA and STOVER DAVID, *The Nanosecond Networlders,* eBook
- GIOVAGNOLI MELISSA, 2000, *Networlding,* Jossey-Bass
- GLADWELL MALCOLM, 2002, *The Tipping Point,* Back Bay Books
- MISNER IVAN, 1996, *Seven Second Marketing,* Bard Press
- MISNER IVAN, 1998, *Business by Referral,* Bard Press
- MISNER IVAN, 1999, *The World's Best Known Marketing Secret,* Bard Press
- MISNER IVAN, 2000, *Masters of Networking,* Bard Press
- MOORE GEOFFREY, 2002, *Crossing the Chasm,* Collins
- MORGEN SHARON DREW, 1999, *Selling with Integrity,* Berkley Trade
- MORGEN SHARON DREW, *Buying Facilitation,* eBook
- NIERENBERG ANDREA, 2002, *Nonstop Networking,* Capital Books
- NORDSTROM KJELL and RIDDERSTRALE JONAS, 2001, *Funky Business,* Financial Times Prentice Hall
- PINK DANIEL, 2005, *A Whole New Mind,* Riverhead
- PIPIJN GREET, 2003, *Durf te leven,* Roularta Books
- POWER THOMAS, 2003, *Networking for Life,* Ecademy Press
- RISNER NIGEL, 2003, *You Had Me at Hello,* Forest Oak Publications
- ROANE SUSAN, 1993, *The Secrets of Savvy Networking,* Warner Books
- ROANE SUSAN, 2000, *How to Work a Room,* Collins
- ROBBINS ANTHONY, *Unleash The Power Within* – CD set
- TRACY BRIAN, *Success Masters Academy* – CD set

# References and Recommended Reading

## *Websites*

*Authorities and bloggers about networking:*

- Donna Fisher: www.donnafisher.com
- Melissa Giovagnoli: www.networlding.com
- Gwen Rhys:www.gwenrhys.com
- Heather White: www.magicof.co.uk
- Will Kintish: kintish.co.uk/networking.htm
- Harvey Mackay: www.mackay.com
- Scott Allen and David Teten: www.onlinebusinessnetworks.com
- Thomas Power: http://www.ecademy.com/user/thomaspower
- Leni Chauvin: www.superstarnetworking.com
- Ivan Misner: www.bni.com
- Andrea Nierenberg: www.selfmarketing.com
- Rhonda Sher: www.2minutenetworker.com
- Scott Ginsberg: www.hellomynameisscott.com
- Julia Hubbel: www.principlednetworking.com
- Gene Hildabrand: www.themasternetworker.com
- Naina Redhu: biznetworking.blogspot.com
- Liz Lynch: www.stealthnetworker.com
- Keith Ferrazzi: nevereatalone.typepad.com
- Robyn Henderson: www.networkingtowin.com.au
- Michael Hughes: http://www.michaeljhughes.com/
- Donna Messer: http://www.connectuscanada.com/
- Heshie Segal: http://www.jetnettingconnection.com/

- Steve Harper: http://www.ripplecentral.com/
- Susan RoAne:
  - Website: www.susanroane.com
  - Blog: susanroane.blogs.com
- Hendrik Deckers: www.hendrikdeckers.com
- Jan Vermeiren:
  - Website: www.networking-coach.com
  - Blog: www.janvermeiren.com

Also check out their eZines!

*Recommended eZines (next to those of the networking authorities):*

- Debra Schmidt, the Loyalty Leader (Customer Focus): www.theloy-altyleader.com
- Fred Gleeck (Marketing): www.fredgleeck.com
- Joe Gracia (Marketing): www.givetogetmarketing.com
- IdeaMarketers (Several topics): www.ideamarketers.com
- International Society for Social Network Analysis (INSNA): www.insna.org
- Internet Marketing Center (Internet Marketing): www.marketingtips.com
- Jim Rohn (Personal Development, Sales): www.jimrohn.com
- Larry Chase Web Digest for Marketers (Marketing): www.wdfm.com
- John Assaraf (Personal Development): www.thestreetkid.com
- Joan Stewart, The Publicity Hound (Public Relations): www.publicityhound.com
- Roy Martina (Personal Development): www.roymartina.com
- Bob Burg (Winning Without Intimidation): www.burg.com

# References and Recommended Reading

*Some of the Online Business Networks*

- Ecademy: www.ecademy.com
- LinkedIn: www.linkedin.com
- Xing: www.Xing.com
- Ryze: www.ryze.com
- Soflow: www.soflow.com
- Spoke: www.spoke.com

*Websites and Blogs about Online Networking*

- entrepreneurs.about.com/od/onlinenetworking
- www.onlinebusinessnetworks.com
- socialsoftware.weblogsinc.com
- www.hendrikdeckers.com

*Tips for Working with Online Business Networks*

- LinkedIn: www.sacredcowdung.com/archives/2005/05/cheaters_guide.html (by Christian Mayaud)
- LinkedIn: dallasblue.com/linkedin.htm (by Marc Freedman)
- Ecademy Citizen's Guide English: www.wings4u2fly.com/getguide.htm (by Jazz Singh)
- Ecademy Citizen's Guide in Dutch (Ecademy Bewoners Gids): users.pandora.be/jean.loyens1/ECG_1nov.pdf (by Jean Loyens)

*6 Degrees of Proximity*

- Small world phenomenon: www.absoluteastronomy.com/encyclopedia/s/sm/small_world_phenomenon.htm
- The Oracle (links between actors): www.cs.virginia.edu/oracle
- Band to Band (links between music bands): bandtoband.com/index.php

- Topmanagement (managers and their network in some countries in Europe): www.topmanagement.be
- Celebrity Relationships Game: www.askmynetwork.com/play

*Referral Clubs*

- BNI: www.bni.com
- BRE: www.brenet.co.uk

*Blogging*

- Demo movie about blogging via Blogger: www.businessownerscoachingclub.com/videos/Blogger-firstblog.html
- Free blog software:
  - Blogger: www.blogger.com
  - Wordpress: www.wordpress.com
  - MSN Spaces: www.msnspaces.com
  - Blog.com: www.blog.com
- Blog software with a subscription fee:
  - Typepad (with 30 day free trial): www.typepad.com
  - Blog.com (upgrade): www.blog.com

*Free RSS Readers:*

- Bloglines: www.bloglines.com
- Newsgator: www.newsgator.com (with the option to integrate the RSS reader in MS Outlook)

*Messaging Tools:*

- MSN Messenger: www.msnmessenger.com
- Yahoo Messenger: messenger.yahoo.com
- AOL Instant Messenger: www.aim.com

- ICQ: www.icq.com (abbreviation for "I seek you")
- Jabber: www.jabber.org
- Skype: www.skype.com

*Advanced Searching on the Web:*

- Google
- Search features: www.google.com/help/features.html
- Options: www.google.com/options/
- Soople (one page dashboard for Google): www.google.com/help/features.html

*Networking Support for Events*

- www.eventscope.co.uk
- www.spotme.ch

# Other Products and Services of the Networking Coach

- Free Networking eCourse: basics from this book (see: www.networking-coach.com)
- CD Let's Connect at an event, 30 immediately applicable networking tips to make every event a success
- Networking Workshops
- Networking Training Courses
- Consulting about How to Stimulate Networking at your Event
- Presentations & Keynote Speeches: several topics
  - Golden Triangle of Networking
  - What's Networking About
  - Networking Attitude
  - Networking for Sales People
  - Networking for Students
  - Networking within a Company
  - Networking for Small Business Owners and Freelancers
  - Networking for Job Seekers
  - Special: Conference Opener
  - Special: Networking Business Theater

Detailed Course Modules and Other Presentation Topics on: www.networking-coach.com

## References:

These organizations already followed a workshop or training course of the Networking Coach:

ADM, Agfa, Agoria, AIB-Vincotte, Alcatel, Alfa Laval, Amelior, Atlas Copco, Belgacom, BMW, BT, Business Netwerk Café, Continental Teves, Corinthia, Creyf 's, Deloitte, Delta Lloyd Bank, Dupont, Egemin, Electrabel, Emotionele Intelligentie Instituut, Ernst & Young, Expectra, Exxon Mobil, Fopas, Gemeente Den Haag, HRSquare, Innotek, Instima, Janssen Farmaceutica, KBC, Kimberly Clark, Levi's, Manager Magazines, Nike, Ogilvy, Optima Financial Planners, Pernod Ricard, Promedia, Provinciale Hogeschool Limburg, Randstad, 237

Real Software, SD Worx, Securex, Siemens, SN Brussels Airlines, Soudal, Telenet, Ter Beke, The House of Marketing, Timesmart, TMP, Unizo, VKW, Vlerick Leuven Management School, VOKA, Vormingsweb and a lot of small business owners and freelancers.

Read the complete list and their testimonials on www.networking-coach.com

## Other links:

- Visit the website of "Let's Connect!" www.letsconnect.be
- Read the blog about networking, "The Networking Coach's Opinion" at: www.janvermeiren.com
- Subscribe to the free newsletter: www.networking-coach.com

**Free Bonus material: Online Networking Power Pack**

- Go to www.LetsConnectBook.com/bonus-pack.html and download your FREE Online Networking Power Pack - including a 10 step strategy guide to network online.

www.ingramcontent.com/pod-product-compliance
Lightning Source LLC
Jackson TN
JSHW020016141224
75386JS00025B/551
*9781600372612*